@bibleintro

a Bible handbook
for the
Twitter generation

CHRIS JUBY

Authentic

Copyright © 2015 Chris Juby

21 20 19 18 17 16 15   7 6 5 4 3 2 1

First published in 2015 by Authentic Media Limited
52 Presley Way, Crownhill, Milton Keynes, MK8 0ES.
authenticmedia.co.uk

British Library Cataloguing in Publication Data
A catalogue record for this book is available from the British Library
ISBN: 978-1-78078-124-2   978-1-78078-259-1 (e-book)

Cover design by Jesus Cordero anointingproductions.com

Printed in Great Britain by CPI Books (UK) Ltd., Croydon, CR0 4YY

'A modern-day, Twitter-friendly shorthand that educates and enriches with both its thoroughness and its simplicity. Refresh your own Scripture reading and study or share it with someone who's never picked up a Bible. *@BibleIntro* is friendly and fun, wherever you are in your journey.'

Rachel Barach – General Manager,
BibleGateway.com

'The Bible offers deep wisdom drawn from ancient wells – but how can today's reader get at it? Chris Juby models a focused way of drilling down into the Bible's depths, and he comes up with fresh and probing insights time and again. How wonderful are the tweets of those who bring good news!'

Dr Richard Briggs – Director of Biblical Studies,
Cranmer Hall, Durham; author, *Reading the Bible Wisely*

'Chris has put his experience summarizing the Bible on Twitter to good use. *@BibleIntro* is an accessible and well-grounded introduction to Scripture. It's a useful handbook for anyone who wants to go deeper with reading the Bible for themselves.'

Stephen Gaukroger – Director,
Clarion Trust International; author; international speaker

'You've never been able to so quickly get a solid overview of the Bible and the good, the bad and the ugly it contains. Juby obviously draws on a deep and passionate knowledge of the material, and clearly hopes both to encourage us back to the original text, and to transformational living.'

Dr Bex Lewis – Director of The BIGBible Project;
author, *Raising Children in a Digital Age*

Acknowledgements

My deepest thanks to those who taught me to love Scripture, and to those who helped me with this book.

My dad used to mark the index page of his Bible each time he finished a book. My mum always has a psalm ready at hand. My pastors in various churches have preached and led with diligent attention to Scripture. And I hope that I have inherited more than just precious books from John Freeman and Brenda Woodward.

I'm grateful to Wes Hill first of all for friendship, but also for helping convince me that summarising the Bible on Twitter was an idea worth taking seriously. I can't believe where it has led!

Thank you to the whole team at Authentic for believing in this book, and particularly to Becky Fawcett who has gone above and beyond.

Thank you to Richard Briggs not just for his kind words of endorsement but also his wise and detailed feedback on the manuscript. The book is much the better for it.

Finally I want to thank my amazing wife Hannah for her unwavering support even when it costs.

I pray that Samuel and Elijah will grow up to love the One whom Scripture reveals.

Chris Juby,
Durham, England

Contents

Contents

Introducing @*BibleIntro*

How did I come to be writing an introduction to the Bible? It's a pretty major task, and I wouldn't put myself forward as a scholar or an expert.

I work on staff at king's church in Durham, so that's a start. And I've been reading and studying Scripture pretty much my whole life. But the story of @*BibleIntro* really began in July 2010, when I was looking for a way to focus my daily Bible reading.

I was already a regular user of the Twitter, and I wondered whether it would be possible to summarize each chapter of the Scripture in 140 characters or less to publish as a series of tweets. I registered the @*BibleSummary* account and got started.

People were enthusiastic about the project straight away, so I sent a short press release to my local paper. To my great surprise, the story was picked up in the media all over the world. Within two weeks I had given dozens of newspaper, TV and radio interviews, and the Twitter account had over ten thousand followers.

I continued summarizing a chapter every day without fail for over three years, and finished in 2013 with thirty thousand followers. It was an incredible journey!

The project had a huge impact on my faith and my understanding of Scripture. And along the way, lots of people have got in touch to say that the summaries have helped with their Bible study too.

I'm very glad to have played a small part in helping the @*BibleSummary* followers to engage with Scripture. But if anything, the response to the summaries has only highlighted how hard it can be to understand what's happening if you just dive into the middle of a book like 1 Chronicles or Jeremiah.

And that's how I came to be writing an introduction to Scripture.

I have two aims for @*BibleIntro*:

Firstly, I want to introduce each book of the Bible in a way that gives people confidence in their own reading and understanding.

Secondly, I want to show how each book fits in with the big picture of Scripture.

The Bible is not just a book of wise sayings; it's the big story of the whole universe – of the God who made us, who loves us, who saves us when we mess things up, who has a future planned for us.

Introducing @*BibleIntro*

Engaging with Scripture is an incredible opportunity for God to speak to us and to transform us. My own life has been changed through studying the Bible, and my hope is that this book will encourage you to experience the same.

As Paul writes to Timothy:

'All Scripture is God-breathed and is useful for teaching, rebuking, correcting and training in righteousness, so that the servant of God may be thoroughly equipped for every good work' (2 Tim. 3:16,17 NIV).

How to Use This Book

Here's what you'll find for each book of the Bible in the pages that follow...

What to expect
Each section starts off with a tweet-length summary of what kind of book it is and what you'll find in it.

Chapters
A number to show how many chapters are in the book.

Key people
I've included a list of the key characters who have written or appear in the book.

Timeline
An infographic to help you to see how each book fits into the big story of Scripture. (The point of the Timeline is not to say when each book was written. Scholars have many varying ideas about that! The Timeline is there to show you where each book fits in the story.)

How to Use This Book

Key passage
I've tried to select the passage that best captures the heart and message of each book. (That's an almost impossible task, and you may well want to suggest a different passage. I'm open to that! Send me a message on Twitter at *@BibleIntro* with your suggestion.)

Chapter summaries
I've included a selection of my *@BibleSummary* tweets to give the overall story of each book. For the shorter books you have the tweets for every chapter; for longer books I've selected a few key chapters. You can see the full collection of summaries by visiting www.biblesummary.info.

Something to take away
I've suggested a key insight, lesson or question based on the central themes of each book.

Please feel free to ask questions about the book or get into conversation via my *@BibleIntro* Twitter account.

THE OLD TESTAMENT

What to expect

The story of Israel. God chooses a people to bless the world. He leads them out of Egypt to the promised land. They appoint kings, build the temple, and rebel against God. He sends them into exile and then restores them.

Books

39

Sections

The Books of Moses – Genesis, Exodus, Leviticus, Numbers, Deuteronomy

The History of Israel – Joshua, Judges, Ruth, 1 & 2 Samuel, 1 & 2 Kings, 1 & 2 Chronicles, Ezra, Nehemiah, Esther

The Books of Wisdom – Job, Psalms, Proverbs, Ecclesiastes, Song of Songs

The Major Prophets – Isaiah, Jeremiah, Lamentations, Ezekiel, Daniel

The Minor Prophets – Hosea, Joel, Amos, Obadiah, Jonah, Micah, Nahum, Habakkuk, Zephaniah, Haggai, Zechariah, Malachi

Timeline

THE BEGINNING · THE PATRIARCHS · IN EGYPT · THE WILDERNESS · PROMISED LAND · THE JUDGES · UNITED KINGDOM · DIVIDED KINGDOM · EXILE IN BABYLON · RETURN FROM EXILE · LIFE OF JESUS · THE EARLY CHURCH · THE END

Genesis

What to expect
Genesis is where everything begins. God creates a good world, humans mess it up, God chooses a people and plans to save us.

Chapters 50

Key people
Adam, Eve, Noah, Abraham, Sarah, Isaac, Jacob, Esau, Joseph, Pharaoh.

Timeline

Key passage
Genesis 1:1–5a

In the beginning, when God created the earth and sky, the earth was without form and not yet useful for anything. Deep waters covered the earth, and darkness covered the water. God's Spirit was moving like a storm over the surface of the water.
Then God said, 'Let there be light!' And light began to shine. He saw the light, and he knew that it was good. Then he separated the light from the darkness. God named the light 'day', and he named the darkness 'night'.

Genesis

Chapter summaries (*@BibleSummary*)

Ch 1: God created the heavens, the earth and everything that lives. He made humankind in his image, and gave them charge over the earth.

Ch 3: The serpent deceived the woman; she and Adam ate from the tree. The earth became cursed, and God sent Adam and Eve out of the garden.

Ch 6: Humankind corrupted the earth with evil. God decided to destroy them. He told Noah to build an ark to be saved from the flood.

Ch 15: The Lord promised Abram an heir and many descendants. Abram believed. He was told that they would be enslaved but would then return.

Ch 22: God told Abraham to sacrifice Isaac. As Abraham obeyed, an angel stopped him. The Lord provided a ram instead and blessed Abraham.

Ch 37: Joseph was Israel's favourite son. He had dreams and his brothers were jealous so they sold him. He was bought by Potiphar in Egypt.

Ch 41: Pharaoh had a dream and called for Joseph to interpret it. The dream predicted a famine. Pharaoh put Joseph in charge of all Egypt.

Ch 50: Pharaoh allowed Joseph to go and bury Jacob. Before Joseph died, he said that God would lead his people back to the promised land.

Something to take away
The God who made the world has chosen us to be his people. Even when we fall away, he has a plan to make things right.

Exodus

What to expect
Exodus picks up the story with the Israelites living as slaves in Egypt. God raises up Moses to lead them back to the promised land.

Chapters 40

Key people
Moses, Aaron, Pharaoh, Bezalel (the master craftsman), the Israelites.

Timeline

THE BEGINNING
THE PATRIARCHS
IN EGYPT
THE WILDERNESS
PROMISED LAND
THE JUDGES
UNITED KINGDOM
DIVIDED KINGDOM
EXILE IN BABYLON
RETURN FROM EXILE
LIFE OF JESUS
THE EARLY CHURCH
THE END

Key passage
Exodus 20:2–6

'I am the Lord your God. I am the one who freed you from the land of Egypt, where you were slaves.

'You must not worship any other gods except me.

'You must not make any idols. Don't make any statues or pictures of anything up in the sky or of anything on the earth or of anything down in the water. Don't worship or serve idols of any kind, because I, the Lord, am your God. I hate my people worshipping other gods. People who sin against me become my enemies, and I will punish them. And I will punish their children, their grandchildren, and even their great-grandchildren. But I will be very kind to people who love me and obey my commands. I will be kind to their families for thousands of generations.'

Exodus

Chapter summaries (*@BibleSummary*)

Ch 2:   Pharaoh's daughter found a Hebrew baby by the river. She named him Moses. When he grew up, Moses killed an Egyptian and fled to Midian.

Ch 3:   Moses saw a burning bush. God told him to lead the Israelites out of Egypt. Moses asked God his name and God said, 'I am who I am.'

Ch 7:   Moses and Aaron went to Pharaoh. Aaron's staff became a snake, then the Lord turned the Nile to blood, but Pharaoh wouldn't listen.

Ch 12:   The Lord told the Israelites to take Passover. That night all the firstborn Egyptians were killed. Pharaoh told the Israelites to go.

Ch 14:   Pharaoh's army caught the Israelites by the sea. The Lord parted the waters and the Israelites crossed. The Egyptian army was drowned.

Ch 20:   'I am the Lord your God.' Honour the Lord above everything. Keep the Sabbath. Honour your parents. Don't do wrong to your neighbours.

Ch 24:   The people said, 'All that the Lord has spoken we will do,' and they offered sacrifices. The Lord told Moses to stay on the mountain.

Ch 32:   While Moses was away the people worshipped a golden calf. Moses pleaded with the Lord for them, but then had three thousand killed.

Ch 40:   Moses set up the Meeting Tent and brought in the Box of the Agreement, as the Lord had ordered. The glory of the Lord filled the Tent.

Something to take away

God saved the Israelites from slavery in Egypt, and he saves us from slavery to sin. He led the Israelites to the promised land, and he is leading us to our eternal home with him.

Leviticus

What to expect
A collection of instructions about how the priests should make sacrifices for sin and how the people should live holy lives before God.

Chapters 27

Key people
Moses, Aaron.

Timeline

THE BEGINNING · THE PATRIARCHS · IN EGYPT · **THE WILDERNESS** · PROMISED LAND · THE JUDGES · UNITED KINGDOM · DIVIDED KINGDOM · EXILE IN BABYLON · RETURN FROM EXILE · LIFE OF JESUS · THE EARLY CHURCH · THE END

Key passage
Leviticus 9:22–24

Then Aaron lifted up his hands towards the people and blessed them. After he finished offering the sin offering, the burnt offering and the fellowship offerings, he came down from the altar.
Moses and Aaron went into the Meeting Tent. They came out and blessed the people. Then the Glory of the LORD appeared to all the people. Fire came out from the LORD and burned the burnt offering and fat on the altar. When all the people saw this, they shouted with joy and then bowed to the ground to show their respect.

Chapter summaries (*@BibleSummary*)

Ch 1: Whoever brings a burnt offering should slaughter a bull, a sheep, a goat or a bird. The priest shall burn it on the altar to the Lord.

Ch 8: Moses gathered the people at the Meeting Tent. He made offerings on the altar and consecrated Aaron and his sons with oil and blood.

Ch 10: Nadab and Abihu offered strange fire, so fire came from the Lord and killed them. Aaron and his other sons stayed at the Meeting Tent.

Ch 16: 'Once a year Aaron shall make atonement for the people. He shall bring one goat as a sin offering and release another as a scapegoat.'

Ch 18: 'Don't have sex with a relative, a woman on her period, your neighbour's wife, another man or an animal. These things defile the land.'

Ch 19: 'Be holy. Keep my Sabbaths. Don't turn to idols. Love your neighbour as yourself. Don't mix livestock. Do no injustice. I am the Lord.'

Ch 25: 'Every seventh year the land shall rest. Every fiftieth year shall be a jubilee, when property shall be restored and slaves released.'

Ch 26: 'If you keep my laws I will give peace in the land and make you fruitful. If not I will scatter you, but I will not break my covenant.'

Something to take away

God wants his people to live holy lives. He has made a way to make things right when we mess up.

Numbers

What to expect
The story continues after the Israelites escape from Egypt. They grumble a lot and end up wandering in the desert for forty years.

Chapters 36

Key people
Moses, Aaron, Balaam (a prophet), the Israelites.

Timeline

THE BEGINNING · THE PATRIARCHS · IN EGYPT · **THE WILDERNESS** · PROMISED LAND · THE JUDGES · UNITED KINGDOM · DIVIDED KINGDOM · EXILE IN BABYLON · RETURN FROM EXILE · LIFE OF JESUS · THE EARLY CHURCH · THE END

Key passage
Numbers 14:20–23

The Lord answered, 'Yes, I will forgive the people as you asked. But I tell you the truth. As surely as I live and as surely as the Glory of the Lord fills the whole earth, I make you this promise: None of the people I led out of Egypt will ever see the land of Canaan. They saw my glory and the great signs that I did in Egypt and in the desert. But they disobeyed me and tested me ten times. I promised their ancestors I would give them that land. But none of those people who turned against me will ever enter that land!'

Chapter summaries (*@BibleSummary*)

Ch 1: The Lord told Moses to count the Israelite armies. The number of men over 20 years old was 603,550. The Levites were not counted.

Ch 7: The leader of each tribe brought a grain offering, a burnt offering, a sin offering and peace offerings. Moses spoke with the Lord.

Ch 11: The people grumbled that they had no meat. The Lord was angry but he sent quails. He put his Spirit on seventy elders to help Moses.

Ch 14: The people grumbled so the Lord said that they would spend forty years in the wilderness. They went up to the land but were defeated.

Ch 20: The Lord told Moses to speak to a rock to produce water but he struck the rock. Edom refused Israel passage. Aaron died at Mount Hor.

Ch 22: Balak sent for Balaam to curse Israel. Balaam's donkey warned him. The angel of the Lord said, 'Go, but speak only what I tell you.'

Ch 31: The Lord told Moses to take vengeance on the Midianites. The Israelites killed the men, burned their cities and divided the spoils.

Ch 33: The Israelites journeyed from Egypt. In the fortieth year Aaron died. They camped by the Jordan and the Lord said, 'Take the land.'

Something to take away
God knows what he's doing. He is faithful even when we grumble about how his plans are working out.

Deuteronomy

What to expect

Moses' last words to the Israelites before he dies. He tells the story of the past forty years and reminds the people of God's covenant.

Chapters 34

Key people
Moses, the Israelites.

Timeline

THE BEGINNING
THE PATRIARCHS
IN EGYPT
THE WILDERNESS
PROMISED LAND
THE JUDGES
UNITED KINGDOM
DIVIDED KINGDOM
EXILE IN BABYLON
RETURN FROM EXILE
LIFE OF JESUS
THE EARLY CHURCH
THE END

Key passage
Deuteronomy 28:1

Now, if you will be careful to obey the Lord your God and follow all his commands that I tell you today, the Lord your God will put you high above all the nations on earth.

Chapter summaries (*@BibleSummary*)

Ch 1: The words of Moses: 'We journeyed from Horeb. You would not go up to take the land, so the Lord said, "This generation will not see it."'

Ch 2: 'We went into the wilderness. Thirty-eight years passed, then the Lord told us to cross by Moab. He delivered Sihon the Amorite to us.'

Ch 5: 'The Lord made his covenant with us: Have no other gods; Keep the Sabbath; Honour your parents. You shall do all that he has commanded.'

Ch 6: 'Hear, O Israel: The Lord our God is one. Love the Lord with all your heart, soul and strength. Teach your children these commandments.'

Ch 8: 'The Lord led you in the wilderness and tested you. He is bringing you into a good land. Do not forget the Lord or you shall perish.'

Ch 12: 'Destroy the high places where the nations worship their gods. You shall bring your offerings at the place that the Lord will choose.'

Ch 17: 'Anyone who breaks the covenant shall be put to death. Go to the priests with hard decisions. Appoint the king that the Lord chooses.'

Ch 26: 'Bring the first fruits of the land to the Lord. Bring a tithe in the third year and say to the Lord, "Look down and bless your people."'

Ch 30: 'When you return to the Lord he will have compassion; he will circumcise your heart. I have set before you life and death. Choose life.'

Deuteronomy

Ch 34: Moses climbed Mount Nebo. There the Lord showed him the promised land. Then Moses died. No prophet has arisen in Israel like Moses.

Something to take away
God's people should remember his faithfulness, teach their children his laws, and trust him for the future.

Joshua

What to expect
After Moses dies, Joshua leads the people of Israel into the promised land. This is the story of Joshua's victories and the division of the land among the tribes.

Chapters 24

Key people
Joshua, the tribes of Israel.

Timeline

Key passage
Joshua 21:43–45

So the LORD kept the promise that he had made to the Israelites and gave the people all the land that he had promised. The people took the land and lived there. And the LORD allowed them to have peace on all sides of their land, just as he had promised their ancestors. None of their enemies defeated them. The LORD allowed the Israelites to defeat every enemy. The LORD kept every promise that he made to the Israelites. There were no promises that he failed to keep. Every promise came true.

Joshua

Chapter summaries (@BibleSummary)

Ch 2: Joshua sent two spies to Jericho. A prostitute called Rahab hid them, so they promised to spare her family. They reported to Joshua.

Ch 6: The Lord said that the army should march around Jericho. On the seventh day they shouted and the walls fell. They destroyed the city.

Ch 11: The kings of the north joined forces to fight against Israel but the Lord gave Joshua victory. So Joshua took the whole land.

Ch 13: Now Joshua was old. The Lord said, 'Divide the remaining land among the tribes.' Moses had given land to Reuben, Gad and Manasseh.

Ch 18: Joshua sent surveyors from the remaining tribes and then divided the land. Benjamin's lot was from Kiriath Jearim to the Dead Sea.

Ch 21: The Israelites gave cities and pasture lands to the Levites. So the Lord gave Israel all the land he had promised to their fathers.

Ch 23: Joshua summoned Israel and said, 'You have seen all that the Lord has done. Hold fast to the Lord or you will perish from the land.'

Something to take away
God keeps his promises. However much we mess things up, he'll get us where he wants us to be.

Judges

What to expect
After the Israelites settle in the promised land they turn away from God. He raises up judges to call the people back.

> **Chapters** 21
>
> **Key people**
> The judges, including Deborah, Gideon and Samson.

Timeline

THE BEGINNING · THE PATRIARCHS · IN EGYPT · THE WILDERNESS · PROMISED LAND · **THE JUDGES** · UNITED KINGDOM · DIVIDED KINGDOM · EXILE IN BABYLON · RETURN FROM EXILE · LIFE OF JESUS · THE EARLY CHURCH · THE END

Key passage
Judges 2:18,19

Many times the enemies of Israel did bad things to them, so the Israelites would cry for help. And each time, the LORD felt sorry for the people and sent a judge to save them from their enemies. The LORD was always with those judges. As long as the judges lived, the Israelites were saved from their enemies. But when each judge died, the Israelites again sinned and started worshipping the false gods. They became worse than their ancestors. The Israelites were very stubborn and refused to change their evil ways.

Judges

Chapter summaries (*@BibleSummary*)

Ch 2: After Joshua's generation died the Israelites served Baals. The Lord sold them to their enemies but raised up judges to deliver them.

Ch 4: Jabin and Sisera oppressed Israel. Deborah sent Barak against them and the Lord routed them. Jael drove a peg through Sisera's head.

Ch 6: The Lord gave the Israelites to Midian. The angel of the Lord told Gideon to save Israel and gave him a sign. Gideon gathered an army.

Ch 8: Gideon defeated Zebah and Zalmunna and punished Succoth and Penuel. He refused to rule Israel. When Gideon died Israel served Baals.

Ch 16: Samson loved Delilah. She had his hair shaved so he lost his strength and was captured. He died pulling down the Philistine temple.

Ch 20: The Israelites gathered to attack Gibeah. The Benjaminites defended the city but they were defeated and only 600 of them survived.

Something to take away

Sometimes we have to stand up for God, even when everyone else is just doing their own thing. God will always raise up leaders to call people back.

Ruth

What to expect
The story of king David's great-grandparents. Ruth entrusts herself to her mother-in-law after her husband dies. She is protected by their kinsman, Boaz.

Chapters 4

Key people
Naomi (the mother-in-law), Ruth, Boaz (the kinsman).

Timeline

THE BEGINNING · THE PATRIARCHS · IN EGYPT · THE WILDERNESS · PROMISED LAND · **THE JUDGES** · UNITED KINGDOM · DIVIDED KINGDOM · EXILE IN BABYLON · RETURN FROM EXILE · LIFE OF JESUS · THE EARLY CHURCH · THE END

Key passage
Ruth 1:16,17

But Ruth said, 'Don't force me to leave you! Don't force me to go back to my own people. Let me go with you. Wherever you go, I will go. Wherever you sleep, I will sleep. Your people will be my people. Your God will be my God. Where you die, I will die, and that is where I will be buried. I ask the Lord to punish me if I don't keep this promise: Only death will separate us.'

Ruth

Chapter summaries (*@BibleSummary*)

Ch 1: Naomi, an Ephraimite, lived in Moab. Her husband and two sons died so she returned to Bethlehem with her daughter-in-law, Ruth.

Ch 2: Naomi had a rich relative named Boaz. Ruth went to glean in his fields. Boaz gave her food and told his men to leave grain for her.

Ch 3: Naomi told Ruth to go and sleep at Boaz's feet. When Boaz awoke, Ruth said, 'You are my kinsman.' Boaz said that he would marry her.

Ch 4: Boaz settled the inheritance with another kinsman and married Ruth. Ruth bore a son, Obed. Obed was father of Jesse, father of David.

Something to take away
Families and relationships matter. Who knows what God might have planned for the people we love?

1 Samuel

What to expect
After the time of judges, the
Israelites demand a king. The
people crown Saul, but God
tells Samuel to anoint David to
replace him.

Chapters 31

Key people
Hannah, Samuel, Eli, Saul,
David, Jonathan.

Timeline

Key passage
1 Samuel 8:6–9

*So the leaders asked for a king to lead them. Samuel thought this was a
bad idea, so he prayed to the Lord. The Lord told Samuel, 'Do what the
people tell you. They have not rejected you. They have rejected me. They
don't want me to be their king. They are doing the same thing they have
always done. I took them out of Egypt, but they left me and served other
gods. They are doing the same to you. So listen to the people and do what
they say. But give them a warning. Tell the people what a king will do to
them. Tell them how a king rules people.'*

1 Samuel

Chapter summaries (@BibleSummary)

Ch 3: The Lord called Samuel. Eli told Samuel to answer, 'Speak, Lord.' The Lord told Samuel that he was about to judge the house of Eli.

Ch 4: The Philistines crushed the Israelites and Eli's sons were killed. When Eli heard the Box of the Agreement had been captured he died.

Ch 8: The elders of Israel asked Samuel to appoint a king. Samuel warned them what it would mean. The Lord told Samuel to give them a king.

Ch 11: The Ammonites attacked Jabesh Gilead. Saul gathered the Israelites and defeated the Ammonites. The people made Saul king at Gilgal.

Ch 16: The Lord sent Samuel to anoint Jesse's son David as king. The Spirit came upon David. Saul sent for David to play the harp for him.

Ch 17: A Philistine champion named Goliath challenged the Israelites. David killed Goliath with a sling and a stone. The Philistines fled.

Ch 18: Jonathan loved David. Saul set David over the army but became jealous and tried to kill him. David married Saul's daughter Michal.

Ch 22: About four hundred men joined David. Saul ordered that all the priests be killed because they helped David. Only Abiathar escaped.

Ch 24: Saul went after David. David cut off a piece of Saul's robe but spared his life. Saul wept and said, 'You shall surely be king.'

Ch 27: David lived among the Philistines to escape Saul. King Achish gave him Ziklag. David secretly raided the land while he lived there.

Ch 31: The Philistines fought Israel. Saul's sons were killed. Saul was badly wounded so he fell on his sword. The Israelites fled.

Something to take away
Other people may be impressed by our appearance, successes and qualifications (or not), but God looks at our hearts.

2 Samuel

What to expect

The highs and lows of king David. He brings the Box of Agreement to Jerusalem, but commits adultery, and has all kinds of trouble with his son Absalom.

Chapters 24

Key people
David, Nathan, Bathsheba, Absalom.

Timeline

Key passage
2 Samuel 7:8–11

'You must say this to my servant David: "This is what the LORD All-Powerful says: I chose you while you were out in the pasture following the sheep. I took you from that job and made you the leader of my people, the Israelites. I have been with you everywhere you went. I have defeated your enemies for you. I will make you one of the most famous people on earth. And I chose a place for my people, the Israelites. I planted the Israelites. I gave them their own place to live so that they will not have to move from place to place any more. In the past, I sent judges to lead my people, but evil people gave them many troubles. That will not happen now. I am giving you peace from all of your enemies. I promise that I will make your family a family of kings."'

Chapter summaries (@*BibleSummary*)

Ch 5: David was anointed king over Israel. He took Jerusalem and the Lord was with him. The Philistines gathered but David defeated them.

Ch 6: David brought the Box of the Agreement from Judah. Uzzah touched it and died. As it came into the city, David danced before the Lord.

Ch 11: David lay with Uriah's wife Bathsheba and she fell pregnant. He told Joab to have Uriah killed in battle. David married Bathsheba.

Ch 13: David's son Amnon sent for his sister Tamar and raped her. Tamar's brother Absalom had his servants kill Amnon and then he fled.

Ch 15: Absalom went to Hebron and sent out spies to proclaim him king. David fled, but he told Zadok and Hushai to return to Jerusalem.

Ch 18: The servants of David defeated Israel. Absalom got stuck in a tree and Joab killed him. Ahimaaz and a Cushite ran to tell David.

Ch 24: David numbered the people of Israel and then regretted it. The Lord sent a plague. David bought Araunah's field and made offerings.

Something to take away

Even if it looks like we're doing well, we need to be careful not to give in to temptation. God can use us despite our faults, but there may be ugly consequences.

1 Kings

What to expect

The story of king Solomon's rule over Israel, and the kings that follow after Israel and Judah divide. The prophet Elijah makes his appearance towards the end.

Chapters 22

Key people
Solomon, Jeroboam, Elijah, Ahab, Jezebel.

Timeline

THE BEGINNING
THE PATRIARCHS
IN EGYPT
THE WILDERNESS
PROMISED LAND
THE JUDGES
UNITED KINGDOM
DIVIDED KINGDOM
EXILE IN BABYLON
RETURN FROM EXILE
LIFE OF JESUS
THE EARLY CHURCH
THE END

Key passage
1 Kings 18:36–39

At about the time for the evening sacrifice, the prophet Elijah approached the altar and prayed, 'Lord, the God of Abraham, Isaac and Jacob, I ask you now to prove that you are the God of Israel and that I am your servant. Show these people that it was you who commanded me to do all these things. Lord, answer my prayer. Show these people that you, Lord, are God and that you are the one who is bringing them back to you.'
Then fire came down from the Lord and burned the sacrifice, the wood, the stones, and the ground around the altar. Then it dried up all the water in the ditch. All the people saw this happen and bowed down to the ground and began saying, 'The Lord is God! The Lord is God!'

Chapter summaries (*@BibleSummary*)

Ch 1:   David was very old. His son Adonijah exalted himself as king. When David heard he told Zadok and Nathan to anoint Solomon as king.

Ch 3:   Solomon married Pharaoh's daughter. He asked the Lord for discernment. Two women came before him and he judged between them wisely.

Ch 6:   Solomon built the Temple. The Lord said, 'If you walk in my ways I will dwell with Israel.' Solomon overlaid the Temple with gold.

Ch 11:   Solomon had many wives and turned to other gods. Ahijah told Jeroboam that the Lord would give him ten of the tribes. Solomon died.

Ch 12:   Rehoboam refused to reduce the labour demands on Israel. So all Israel except Judah made Jeroboam king. Jeroboam made golden calves.

Ch 16:   Elah ruled Israel and did evil. Zimri killed Elah but Israel made Omri king. Omri did evil. Ahab ruled and began to worship Baal.

Ch 18:   Elijah went to Ahab and challenged the prophets of Baal. Baal gave no answer but the Lord answered Elijah with fire. Then rain fell.

Ch 21:   Naboth would not sell his vineyard, so Jezebel had him killed. Elijah said to Ahab, 'Dogs will lick up your blood and eat Jezebel.'

Something to take away
We need God's wisdom to know how to use whatever power we have. If we don't keep seeking God, we will end up making a huge mess.

2 Kings

What to expect

Stories about the prophet Elisha, and the (mostly evil) kings of Israel and Judah, until the Babylonians take the Israelites into exile.

Chapters 25

Key people
Elisha, Ahaziah, Hezekiah, Josiah.

Timeline

THE BEGINNING · THE PATRIARCHS · IN EGYPT · THE WILDERNESS · PROMISED LAND · THE JUDGES · UNITED KINGDOM · **DIVIDED KINGDOM** · **EXILE IN BABYLON** · RETURN FROM EXILE · LIFE OF JESUS · THE EARLY CHURCH · THE END

Key passage
2 Kings 18:5–7a

Hezekiah trusted in the LORD, the God of Israel. There was no one like Hezekiah among all the kings of Judah before him or after him. He was very faithful to the LORD and did not stop following him. He obeyed the commands that the LORD had given to Moses. The LORD was with Hezekiah, so he was successful in everything he did.

Chapter summaries (@*BibleSummary*)

Ch 2: Elisha followed Elijah. A chariot of fire appeared and Elijah went up to heaven. Elisha took Elijah's mantle and divided the waters.

Ch 3: Israel, Judah and Edom went to fight Moab. Elisha said, 'The Lord will send water and give you Moab.' The Moabites were defeated.

Ch 6: The king of Aram sent an army to capture Elisha but the Lord blinded them. Ben-Hadad besieged Samaria and there was a great famine.

Ch 12: Joash ruled in Jerusalem and did what was right. The priests collected money to repair the Temple. Joash was killed by his servants.

Ch 16: Ahaz ruled Judah and did evil. Aram and Israel attacked Judah so Ahaz sent a tribute to the king of Assyria. Ahaz set up an altar.

Ch 18: Hezekiah ruled Judah and did right. The Assyrians surrounded Jerusalem. Rabshakeh said, 'Don't listen to Hezekiah. Come out to me.'

Ch 19: Hezekiah prayed, 'O Lord, save us.' Isaiah said, 'The Lord says: I will defend the city.' That night the Assyrians were struck dead.

Ch 21: Manasseh ruled in Jerusalem and did evil. The Lord said, 'I will bring disaster on Jerusalem and Judah.' Amon ruled and did evil.

Ch 22: Josiah ruled and did right. He had the law read out and tore his robes. Huldah said, 'The Lord says: You will be buried in peace.'

2 Kings

Ch 25: Nebuchadnezzar besieged Jerusalem. Nebuzaradan burned the Temple and took the people into exile. Evil Merodach released Jehoiachin.

Something to take away

It's a blessing when the people in charge are serving the Lord, but that won't always be the case. We need to trust that God is at work whatever happens.

1 Chronicles

What to expect

1 Chronicles starts with nine chapters of genealogy, then repeats many of the stories of David from 2 Samuel, emphasizing the importance of praise.

Chapters 29

Key people
David, Solomon, Joab.

Timeline

THE BEGINNING
THE PATRIARCHS
IN EGYPT
THE WILDERNESS
PROMISED LAND
THE JUDGES
UNITED KINGDOM
DIVIDED KINGDOM
EXILE IN BABYLON
RETURN FROM EXILE
LIFE OF JESUS
THE EARLY CHURCH
THE END

Key passage
1 Chronicles 11:3

All the leaders of Israel came to king David at the town of Hebron. David made an agreement with them in Hebron before the LORD. The leaders anointed David. That made him king over Israel. The LORD had promised through Samuel that this would happen.

1 Chronicles

Chapter summaries (*@BibleSummary*)

Ch 1: Adam, Seth, Noah, Shem, Eber, Abraham; Abraham's sons were Isaac and Ishmael; Isaac's sons were Esau and Israel. Kings ruled in Edom.

Ch 3: David had six sons at Hebron, four by Bathsheba and nine others. Solomon's line led to Jehoiachin, and then to the sons of Elioenai.

Ch 9: Jerusalem was resettled by Judah, Benjamin, Ephraim and Manasseh; there were priests and Levite gatekeepers. Kish was father of Saul.

Ch 11: The elders anointed David king. David's mighty men included the three who brought him water from Bethlehem. Abishai led the thirty.

Ch 15: David told the Levites to carry the Box of the Agreement into the city of David. Heman, Asaph and Ethan were the musicians.

Ch 19: The king of Ammon humiliated David's servants and hired the Arameans for war. Joab defeated them and David defeated king Hadadezer.

Ch 28: David assembled the leaders and said, 'The Lord has chosen Solomon to build his house.' He gave Solomon the plans for the Temple.

Ch 29: The leaders gave offerings. David prayed, 'Yours is the kingdom, O Lord. Of your own have we given you.' David died at an old age.

Something to take away

Everyone matters in the story of God. Maybe you feel as if no one knows who you are, but God knows you. You have a part to play.

2 Chronicles

What to expect

2 Chronicles retells many of the stories of king Solomon's reign and the kings of Judah from 1 and 2 Kings until the Babylonians take the Israelites into exile.

Chapters 36

Key people
Solomon, Jeroboam, Jehoshaphat, Hezekiah, Nebuchadnezzar.

Timeline

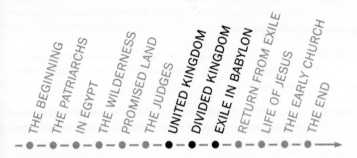

THE BEGINNING
THE PATRIARCHS
IN EGYPT
THE WILDERNESS
PROMISED LAND
THE JUDGES
UNITED KINGDOM
DIVIDED KINGDOM
EXILE IN BABYLON
RETURN FROM EXILE
LIFE OF JESUS
THE EARLY CHURCH
THE END

Key passage
2 Chronicles 7:1–3

When Solomon finished praying, fire came down from the sky and burned up the burnt offering and the sacrifices. The Glory of the Lord filled the Temple. The priests could not enter the Lord's Temple because the Glory of the Lord filled it. When all the Israelites saw the fire come down from heaven and the Glory of the Lord on the Temple, they bowed down on the pavement with their faces low to the ground. They worshipped and thanked the Lord, singing,
> *'The Lord is good.*
> *His faithful love will last forever.'*

2 Chronicles

Chapter summaries (*@BibleSummary*)

Ch 1: Solomon made offerings. God said, 'What shall I give you?' Solomon said, 'Wisdom to rule this people.' So Solomon ruled over Israel.

Ch 3: Solomon started work on the Temple. He built the portico, the main hall, the Most Holy Place, two cherubim, the veil and two pillars.

Ch 5: The Box of the Agreement was placed in the Most Holy Place. The singers praised the Lord and the glory of the Lord filled the Temple.

Ch 7: Fire came from heaven and the Israelites worshipped. The Lord said to Solomon, 'If you walk in my ways I will establish your throne.'

Ch 9: The queen of Sheba came to test Solomon and gave him gold and spices. Solomon excelled all the kings of the earth. Then he died.

Ch 12: Rehoboam was unfaithful to the Lord so Shishak attacked Jerusalem. Rehoboam humbled himself and the anger of the Lord turned away.

Ch 17: Jehoshaphat became king and was devoted to the Lord. He sent his officials to teach the law. He grew greater and built fortresses.

Ch 21: Jehoram ruled and did evil. Elijah wrote saying, 'The Lord will send a plague.' The Lord struck Jehoram with a disease and he died.

Ch 29: Hezekiah became king and did right. He told the Levites to cleanse the Temple. He assembled the officials and they made offerings.

Ch 32: Sennacherib besieged Judah. Hezekiah and Isaiah cried out to the Lord and the Assyrians were struck dead. Hezekiah had great riches.

Ch 36: Jehoahaz, Jehoiakim, Jehoiachin and Zedekiah ruled. Then Nebuchadnezzar burned the Temple and took Judah captive for seventy years.

Something to take away

It may feel as if the big news stories of our day are the be-all, and end-all, but God takes the longer view. Through the ups and downs of history, God is working his purposes out.

Ezra

What to expect
After the Israelites have been in exile for seventy years, they are allowed to return to their land. Ezra leads the rebuilding of the Temple.

Chapters 10

Key people
Cyrus, Zerubbabel, Ezra.

Timeline

THE BEGINNING · THE PATRIARCHS · IN EGYPT · THE WILDERNESS · PROMISED LAND · THE JUDGES · UNITED KINGDOM · DIVIDED KINGDOM · EXILE IN BABYLON · RETURN FROM EXILE · LIFE OF JESUS · THE EARLY CHURCH · THE END

Key passage
Ezra 1:2,3

From king Cyrus of Persia:

The Lord, the God of heaven, gave all the kingdoms on earth to me. And he chose me to build a temple for him at Jerusalem in the country of Judah. If any of God's people are living among you, I pray that God will bless them. You must let them go to Jerusalem in the country of Judah. You must let them go and build the Temple of the Lord, the God of Israel, the God who is in Jerusalem.

Chapter summaries (*@BibleSummary*)

Ch 1: Cyrus said, 'Let the Lord's people go up to Jerusalem and rebuild the Temple.' He gave the articles from the Temple to Sheshbazzar.

Ch 3: The Israelites made regular offerings. When the builders laid the foundation of the Temple, the Levites sang praise to the Lord.

Ch 4: Enemies hindered the work in Judah. Rehum wrote to Artaxerxes: 'Jerusalem is a rebellious city.' So Artaxerxes stopped the building.

Ch 6: Darius issued a decree: 'The cost of the Temple shall come from the treasury.' The Temple was completed and the Israelites celebrated.

Ch 8: I assembled the family heads from Babylon and gave the gifts for the Temple to the Levites. We came to Jerusalem and made offerings.

Ch 10: The Israelites wept. They all assembled and Ezra said, 'Separate from your foreign wives.' The family heads investigated the matter.

Something to take away

Sometimes God uses unexpected people to achieve his purposes – even the 'bad guys'. Just when we think we know how he works, he does something that completely surprises us.

Nehemiah

What to expect
Nehemiah overcomes much opposition to lead the Israelites in rebuilding the walls of Jerusalem after they return from exile in Babylon.

Chapters 13

Key people
Nehemiah, Ezra.

Timeline

THE BEGINNING · THE PATRIARCHS · IN EGYPT · THE WILDERNESS · PROMISED LAND · THE JUDGES · UNITED KINGDOM · DIVIDED KINGDOM · EXILE IN BABYLON · RETURN FROM EXILE · LIFE OF JESUS · THE EARLY CHURCH · THE END

Key passage
Nehemiah 2:17

Then I said to them, 'You can see the trouble we have here: Jerusalem is a pile of ruins, and its gates have been burned with fire. Come, let's rebuild the wall of Jerusalem. Then we will not be ashamed any more.'

Chapter summaries (*@BibleSummary*)

Ch 2: The king granted my request to go and rebuild Jerusalem. Sanballat was displeased. I inspected the walls and said, 'Let us rebuild.'

Ch 3: The priests rebuilt the Sheep Gate, the Tekoites made repairs, Jedaiah repaired opposite his house, Meremoth repaired another section.

Ch 4: Sanballat ridiculed us and plotted to attack Jerusalem. So we prayed and posted a guard. The builders carried swords as they worked.

Ch 8: The people gathered and Ezra read the law. Nehemiah said, 'This day is holy. Do not mourn.' The people held the Festival of Shelters.

Ch 12: All the Levites and leaders gathered to dedicate the wall. They made offerings and rejoiced. Men were appointed over the storerooms.

Something to take away
Community matters. As we get on with our own lives, jobs and families, don't forget to work with others for the common good.

Esther

What to expect

The story of a young girl's courage in a time of crisis after the exile in Babylon. Haman sets out to destroy the Jews, but his plan spectacularly backfires.

Chapters 10

Key people
Esther (our heroine), Mordecai (her wise uncle), Xerxes (the king), Haman (the villain).

Timeline

THE BEGINNING · THE PATRIARCHS · IN EGYPT · THE WILDERNESS · PROMISED LAND · THE JUDGES · UNITED KINGDOM · DIVIDED KINGDOM · EXILE IN BABYLON · **RETURN FROM EXILE** · LIFE OF JESUS · THE EARLY CHURCH · THE END

Key passage
Esther 4:12–14

Then Esther's message was given to Mordecai. When he got her message, Mordecai sent his answer back: 'Esther, don't think that just because you live in the king's palace you will be the only Jew to escape. If you keep quiet now, help and freedom for the Jews will come from another place. But you and your father's family will all die. And who knows, maybe you have been chosen to be the queen for such a time as this.'

Chapter summaries (*@BibleSummary*)

Ch 2: Mordecai raised Esther. She was taken into the king's harem and was chosen as queen. Mordecai told Esther of a plot against the king.

Ch 3: Xerxes promoted Haman, but Mordecai would not bow to him. Haman asked to destroy the Jews. The king gave his seal for the decree.

Ch 4: Mordecai asked Esther to plead with the king. Esther said, 'Hold a fast. I will go to the king against the law, and if I die, I die.'

Ch 5: Esther won favour with the king. She said, 'Let the king and Haman come to a feast tomorrow.' Haman built a gallows to hang Mordecai.

Ch 6: That night the king read about the plot against him. Haman came to ask about hanging Mordecai. The king told Haman to honour Mordecai.

Ch 7: At the feast, the king asked Esther, 'What is your request?' She said, 'My people have been sold by Haman.' The king had Haman hanged.

Ch 8: The king gave his ring to Mordecai. Mordecai sent letters to the provinces allowing the Jews to defend themselves. The Jews rejoiced.

Ch 9: On the day of the king's decree, the Jews destroyed their enemies. Mordecai wrote to all the Jews and established the Feast of Purim.

Something to take away
Maybe God has a special purpose for you in your school, your workplace, your position in the world. Do you have the courage to fulfil it?

Job

What to expect
A long conversation about suffering. Job is a righteous man who loses everything. His friends arrive to comfort him, but they end up arguing about who is to blame.

Chapters 42

Key people
Job; his three friends Eliphaz, Bildad and Zophar; Elihu.

Timeline

THE BEGINNING · THE PATRIARCHS · IN EGYPT · THE WILDERNESS · PROMISED LAND · THE JUDGES · UNITED KINGDOM · DIVIDED KINGDOM · EXILE IN BABYLON · RETURN FROM EXILE · LIFE OF JESUS · THE EARLY CHURCH · THE END

Key passage
Job 1:8–12a

Then the Lord said to Satan, 'Have you noticed my servant Job? There is no one on earth like him. He is a good, faithful man. He respects God and refuses to do evil.'

Satan answered the Lord, 'But Job has a good reason to respect you. You always protect him, his family and everything he has. You have blessed him and made him successful in everything he does. He is so wealthy that his herds and flocks are all over the country. But if you were to destroy everything he has, I promise you that he would curse you to your face.'

The Lord said to Satan, 'All right, do whatever you want with anything that he has, but don't hurt Job himself.'

Chapter summaries (@*BibleSummary*)

Ch 1: Job was blameless. The Lord allowed Satan to test him. Job's servants and children were killed. He tore his robes and worshipped.

Ch 3: Job said, 'Curse the day I was born! Why did I not die at birth? Why is light given to him who suffers? I have no rest, only turmoil.'

Ch 4: Eliphaz said, 'Will you become impatient? When did the innocent ever perish? I heard a voice: "Can a man be more righteous than God?"'

Ch 8: Bildad said, 'Does God pervert justice? Learn from past generations. He will not reject the blameless, nor will he uphold evildoers.'

Ch 9: Job said, 'How can a man dispute with God? His power is vast! But he destroys the innocent. If only there were a mediator between us!'

Ch 11: Zophar said, 'Should your babble go unanswered? God exacts less than your guilt deserves! Reach out to him and you will find hope.'

Ch 15: Eliphaz said, 'Your own mouth condemns you! Why do you turn against God? The wicked will be like a vine stripped of unripe grapes.'

Ch 19: Job said, 'How long will you torment me? God counts me as an enemy. My closest friends abhor me. But I know that my redeemer lives!'

Ch 31: 'Does God not see my ways? Have I lied? Have I refused to help the poor? Have I put my trust in money? Let the Almighty answer me!'

Job

Ch 32: Elihu was angry with Job and his three friends. He said, 'I am young, but it is not only the old who are wise. I will have my say.'

Ch 35: 'Even if you are righteous, what do you give to God? He does not answer because of the pride of evil men. You must wait for him!'

Ch 38: Then the Lord said, 'I will question you. Where were you when I founded the earth? Who enclosed the sea? Can you bind the Pleiades?'

Ch 40: Job said, 'I have no answer.' The Lord said, 'Will you condemn me? Behold now Behemoth, which I made. Can anyone pierce his nose?'

Ch 42: Job said, 'I repent in ashes.' The Lord said to Eliphaz, 'You have not spoken rightly of me, as Job has.' He restored Job's fortunes.

Something to take away
Life is not as simple as 'you get what you deserve'. If you're suffering, don't stop asking God about it. If your friend is suffering, you should probably listen more than you talk.

Psalms

What to expect

Israel's hymnbook (in fact, five of them). Psalms were sung in the Temple and used in prayer and personal worship.

Chapters 150

Key people
Seventy-three of the psalms are attributed to David, others are linked to the sons of Asaph, the sons of Korah, Solomon and Moses.

Timeline

THE BEGINNING · THE PATRIARCHS · IN EGYPT · THE WILDERNESS · PROMISED LAND · THE JUDGES · **UNITED KINGDOM** · **DIVIDED KINGDOM** · **EXILE IN BABYLON** · RETURN FROM EXILE · LIFE OF JESUS · THE EARLY CHURCH · THE END

Key passage
Psalm 96:1–4a

Sing a new song to the LORD!
   Let the whole world sing to the LORD!
Sing to the LORD and praise his name!
   Tell the good news every day about how he saves us!
Tell all the nations how wonderful he is!
   Tell people everywhere about the amazing things he does.
The LORD is great and worthy of praise.

Psalms

Chapter summaries (@*BibleSummary*)

Ps 1:   Blessed is the man who does not walk with the wicked, whose delight is in the law of the Lord. He is like a tree planted by the water.

Ps 8:   O Lord, how majestic is your name in all the earth! What is man that you care for him? Yet you have crowned him with glory and honour.

Ps 23:   The Lord is my shepherd. He leads me in paths of righteousness. I will fear no evil. I will dwell in the house of the Lord for ever.

Ps 40:   I waited patiently for the Lord. He drew me up from the pit. I delight to do your will, O God. My heart fails me, but you are my help.

Ps 51:   Have mercy on me, O God! Cleanse me from my sin. Do not cast me away from your presence. A broken heart, O God, you will not despise.

Ps 80:   Hear us, O Shepherd of Israel! How long will you be angry? Restore us, O God. Watch over the vine that you planted. Restore us, O God.

Ps 96:   Sing to the Lord! Declare his glory among the nations. Worship the Lord in holy splendour. He will judge the world in righteousness.

Ps 103:   Bless the Lord, O my soul. He forgives all your iniquity. He has compassion on those who fear him. Bless the Lord, all his works!

Ps 121:   I lift up my eyes to the hills; my help comes from the Lord. He who keeps you will not slumber. The Lord will keep you from all evil.

Ps 133: How good it is when brothers live together in unity! It is like precious oil upon the head. There the Lord commanded his blessing.

Ps 137: By the rivers of Babylon, we wept when we remembered Zion. How can we sing the Lord's song? O Babylon, happy the one who repays you!

Ps 150: Praise the Lord! Praise him with trumpet and strings! Praise him with loud cymbals! Let everything that has breath praise the Lord!

Something to take away

It's never the wrong time to worship God. Whatever we're going through, God is still worthy of our praise.

Proverbs

What to expect
A meditation on wisdom and a collection of wise sayings.

Chapters 31

Key people
Most of the proverbs are attributed to Solomon.

Timeline

THE BEGINNING · THE PATRIARCHS · IN EGYPT · THE WILDERNESS · PROMISED LAND · THE JUDGES · **UNITED KINGDOM** · DIVIDED KINGDOM · EXILE IN BABYLON · RETURN FROM EXILE · LIFE OF JESUS · THE EARLY CHURCH · THE END

Key passage
Proverbs 2:1–5

My son, pay attention to what I say. Remember my commands. Listen to wisdom, and do your best to understand. Ask for good judgement. Cry out for understanding. Look for wisdom like silver. Search for it like hidden treasure. If you do this, you will understand what it means to respect the LORD, and you will come to know God.

Chapter summaries (@*BibleSummary*)

Ch 2: My son, apply your heart to understanding. For the Lord gives wisdom. It will save you from the way of evil, and from the adulteress.

Ch 8: Wisdom cries aloud: 'My mouth speaks truth. The Lord brought me forth at the beginning of his works. Whoever finds me finds life.'

Ch 10: A wise son makes a glad father. Love covers all offences. With many words, sin is not lacking. The righteous will never be uprooted.

Ch 14: The talk of fools is a rod for their backs. Even in laughter the heart may ache. Those who oppress the poor insult their Maker.

Ch 19: Wealth makes friends. A false witness will not go unpunished. A good wife is from the Lord. Whoever helps the poor lends to the Lord.

Ch 22: A good name is better than riches. Train a child and he will not go astray. Incline your ear and apply your heart to my teaching.

Ch 26: As a dog returns to its vomit, so a fool repeats his folly. Without gossip a quarrel dies down. Whoever digs a pit will fall into it.

Ch 28: Better to be poor and honest than crooked and rich. Whoever confesses sins will find mercy. Whoever trusts in the Lord will prosper.

Ch 31: Speak up for the speechless. Who can find an excellent wife? She buys a field, she makes garments, she watches over her household.

Something to take away

Some of these Proverbs can be directly applied to life today; others can't so easily. But we should seek God's wisdom about every part of life.

Ecclesiastes

What to expect
A kind of philosophical journal. The world-weary Teacher reports on his experiences with work, women, wealth and wisdom.

Chapters 12

Key people
The Teacher.

Timeline

THE BEGINNING · THE PATRIARCHS · IN EGYPT · THE WILDERNESS · PROMISED LAND · THE JUDGES · **UNITED KINGDOM** · DIVIDED KINGDOM · EXILE IN BABYLON · RETURN FROM EXILE · LIFE OF JESUS · THE EARLY CHURCH · THE END

Key passage
Ecclesiastes 1:2,3

Everything is so meaningless. The Teacher says that it is all a waste of time! Do people really gain anything from all the hard work they do in this life?

Chapter summaries (*@BibleSummary*)

Ch 1: Everything is meaningless! There is nothing new under the sun. I applied my heart to know wisdom, but much wisdom brings much sorrow.

Ch 2: I built houses, gathered possessions and sought pleasure. It was meaningless! The wise die like the foolish. I despaired of my toil.

Ch 3: There is a time for everything: to live, to die, to mourn, to dance. It is the gift of God that man should find pleasure in his work.

Ch 5: Do not make rash vows before God. The lover of money never has enough. What is gained by toil? It is good to find enjoyment in life.

Ch 9: The same fate comes to all. A living dog is better than a dead lion. Enjoy the days of your vain life. Wisdom is better than strength.

Ch 12: Remember your Creator in your youth, before the days of trouble come. Everything is meaningless! Fear God and keep his commandments.

Something to take away

Even if you're tired, jaded and cynical, the Bible can speak to you and for you. In the end God will be the judge.

Song of Songs

What to expect
A love poem, telling the story of a bride and her lover.

Chapters 8

Key people
The Lover, the Beloved and the women of Jerusalem all take parts in a kind of play.

Timeline

Key passage
Song of Songs 8:6,7

Keep me near you like a seal you wear over your heart,
*   like a signet ring you wear on your hand.*
Love is as strong as death.
*   Passion is as strong as the grave.*
Its sparks become a flame,
*   and it grows to become a great fire!*
A flood cannot put out love.
*   Rivers cannot drown love.*
Would people despise a man for giving
*   everything he owns for love?*

Chapter summaries (*@BibleSummary*)

Ch 1: Let him kiss me! I am dark and lovely. Tell me, where do you pasture your flock? Follow the tracks, my love. Behold, you are beautiful.

Ch 2: She is a lily among thorns. He is an apple tree in the wood. Here he comes, leaping on the mountains. My beloved is mine and I am his.

Ch 4: You are beautiful, my love! Your eyes are doves, your breasts are like fawns. My bride is a garden. Let my beloved come to his garden.

Ch 6: Where has your beloved gone? He has gone to his garden. You are beautiful, my love. Fair as the moon, awesome as an army with banners.

Ch 8: Do not awaken love until it pleases. Love is as strong as death. Solomon had a vineyard, but mine is my own. Make haste, my beloved!

Something to take away

Our love lives are an important part of who God has made us. But notice the patience as well as the passion in the Song of Songs. The repeated advice is that we 'do not awaken love until it is ready'.

Isaiah

What to expect
One of the longest books of prophecy. Jerusalem was not the holy city it should have been. God will judge them and then send his Servant to save them.

Chapters 66

Key people
Isaiah, Hezekiah.

Timeline

Key passage
Isaiah 1:27,28

God is good and does what is right, so he will rescue Zion and the people who come back to him. But all the criminals and sinners will be destroyed. Those who stopped following the Lord will be removed.

Chapter summaries (*@BibleSummary*)

Ch 1: The Lord has spoken: I raised children but they have rebelled. Wash yourselves. I will smelt away your dross. Zion shall be redeemed.

Ch 2: The mountain of the Lord will be established. On that day the pride of men will be humbled. They will flee the splendour of the Lord.

Ch 6: I saw the Lord seated on high. A seraph brought a coal to my lips. The Lord said, 'Who will go for us?' I said, 'Here am I; send me!'

Ch 9: A child is born to us. His government will increase forever. The Lord will raise the enemies of Israel. His anger has not turned away.

Ch 11: A shoot will come up from Jesse. He will judge with righteousness. The wolf will live with the lamb. The Lord will gather his people.

Ch 14: The Lord will again choose Israel. How you are fallen, O Lucifer! You will be cast away like a trampled corpse. Wail, O Philistia!

Ch 24: Behold, the Lord lays the earth waste. Its people are held guilty. Fear and pit and snare await you. The Lord of hosts will reign.

Ch 30: Woe to the stubborn children who seek help from Egypt! The Lord will wait to show mercy. The voice of the Lord will shatter Assyria.

Ch 36: The king of Assyria came against Judah. His commander said, 'Do not listen to Hezekiah. Have any of the gods delivered their lands?'

Isaiah

Ch 40: Comfort, comfort my people. A voice cries: 'Prepare the way of the Lord!' He is the everlasting God. He gives strength to the weary.

Ch 52: Awake, O Zion! How beautiful are those who bring good news. The Lord has redeemed Jerusalem. Behold, my Servant will be lifted up.

Ch 61: The Spirit of the Lord is on me. He has sent me to proclaim freedom. My people will inherit a double portion. I delight in the Lord.

Ch 66: Listen! The Lord is repaying his enemies. Rejoice with Jerusalem and be comforted. All flesh will worship before me, says the Lord.

Something to take away

Even through Israel's unfaithfulness, God was planning to send a Saviour. He saves us through Jesus' suffering on the cross.

Jeremiah

What to expect

A (very) long book of prophecy. Judah is about to be overthrown by the Babylonians. Rather than saving them, God is actually using their enemies to punish his people.

Chapters 52

Key people
Jeremiah, Nebuchadnezzar, Zedekiah.

Timeline

THE BEGINNING · THE PATRIARCHS · IN EGYPT · THE WILDERNESS · PROMISED LAND · THE JUDGES · UNITED KINGDOM · **DIVIDED KINGDOM** · **EXILE IN BABYLON** · RETURN FROM EXILE · LIFE OF JESUS · THE EARLY CHURCH · THE END

Key passage
Jeremiah 31:31–34

This is what the LORD said, 'The time is coming when I will make a new agreement with the family of Israel and with the family of Judah. It will not be like the agreement I made with their ancestors. I made that agreement when I took them by the hand and brought them out of Egypt. I was their master, but they broke that agreement.' This message is from the LORD.

'In the future I will make this agreement with the people of Israel.' This message is from the LORD. 'I will put my teachings in their minds, and I will write them on their hearts. I will be their God, and they will be my people. People will not have to teach their neighbours and relatives to know the LORD, because all people, from the least important to the most important, will know me.' This message is from the LORD. 'I will forgive them for the evil things they did. I will not remember their sins.'

Jeremiah

Chapter summaries (@*BibleSummary*)

Ch 1: The Lord said to me: 'I appointed you as a prophet to the nations. Don't be afraid. I am calling the northern kingdoms against Judah.'

Ch 2: 'My people have exchanged their glory for idols. You have all rebelled against me. Now I will bring you to judgement.'

Ch 5: 'Israel and Judah have been unfaithful to me. I am bringing a distant nation against you. Your sins have deprived you of good.'

Ch 18: The Lord said: 'Go to the potter. You are clay in my hand O Israel. My people have forgotten me.' O Lord, they have dug a pit for me.

Ch 23: 'I will raise up a good branch,' says the Lord. 'The prophets fill you with false hopes. I did not speak, yet they have prophesied.'

Ch 31: 'Sing with joy for Jacob! Return to your cities. I will make a new covenant with Israel,' says the Lord. 'I will put my law in them.'

Ch 37: Zedekiah became king. I said: 'Do not think the Babylonians will leave us.' Irijah arrested me. Zedekiah gave me bread.

Ch 39: Babylon besieged Jerusalem and captured Zedekiah. They took the people into exile. Nebuchadnezzar said, 'Do not harm Jeremiah.'

Ch 51: The Lord says: 'I will send a destroyer against Babylon. I will repay them for the evil done in Zion. Read these words in Babylon.'

Something to take away
God's judgement is painful. The only thing we can do is throw ourselves on his mercy.

Lamentations

What to expect
A poem mourning the destruction
of Jerusalem by the Babylonians.

Chapters 5

Key people
Jeremiah.

Timeline

THE BEGINNING
THE PATRIARCHS
IN EGYPT
THE WILDERNESS
PROMISED LAND
THE JUDGES
UNITED KINGDOM
DIVIDED KINGDOM
EXILE IN BABYLON
RETURN FROM EXILE
LIFE OF JESUS
THE EARLY CHURCH
THE END

Key passage
Lamentations 1:21

Listen to me, I am groaning.
    I have no one to comfort me.
All my enemies have heard of my trouble.
    They are happy that you did this to me.
You said there would be a time of punishment.
    You said you would punish my enemies.
Now do what you promised.
    Let my enemies be like I am now.'

Lamentations

Chapter summaries (*@BibleSummary*)

Ch 1: How lonely sits the city! Judah has gone into exile. 'O Lord, I am despised. Is any sorrow like mine? There is no one to comfor me.'

Ch 4: The holy stones lie scattered. The children beg for food. The Lord has poured out his fierce anger. O Zion, your punishmen will end.

Ch 5: Look, O Lord, and see our disgrace! We have become orphans Slaves rule over us. But you, O Lord, reign forever. Restore us a of old!

Something to take away

There's a time to simply grieve when tragedy strikes. Even if we know that God will make things better, that doesn't take away the sadness c the moment.

Ezekiel

What to expect

Another long book of prophecy about the exile in Babylon. Ezekiel is full of extraordinary visions and prophecies against Israel and the nations. Is there any hope for Israel after God's judgement?

Chapters 48

Key people
Ezekiel, Nebuchadnezzar.

Timeline

THE BEGINNING · THE PATRIARCHS · IN EGYPT · THE WILDERNESS · PROMISED LAND · THE JUDGES · UNITED KINGDOM · DIVIDED KINGDOM · **EXILE IN BABYLON** · RETURN FROM EXILE · LIFE OF JESUS · THE EARLY CHURCH · THE END

Key passage
Ezekiel 37:4–6

Then he said to me, 'Speak to these bones for me. Tell them, "Dry bones, listen to the word of the Lord! This is what the Lord God says to you: I will cause breath to come into you, and you will come to life! I will put sinew and muscles on you, and I will cover you with skin. Then I will put breath in you, and you will come back to life! Then you will know that I am the Lord."'

Ezekiel

Chapter summaries (*@BibleSummary*)

Ch 1: I saw visions of God. Out of a storm came four creatures. I saw wheels within wheels. Above them was a throne and the figure of a man.

Ch 2: He said to me: 'Son of man, stand up.' The Spirit entered me. He said: 'I send you to rebel Israel.' Before me was a scroll of woe.

Ch 6: 'Son of man, prophesy against the mountains of Jerusalem. The slain shall lie among their idols. They will know that I am the Lord.'

Ch 14: The elders came to me. The Lord said: 'They have set up idols in their hearts. Even Noah, Daniel and Job could only save themselves.'

Ch 16: 'Jerusalem, I made you flourish. But you played the whore. I will gather your lovers against you. Yet I will remember my covenant.'

Ch 26: 'Tyre jeered at Jerusalem so I will make her a bare rock. Nebuchadnezzar will lay siege to you. I will bring you to a dreadful end.'

Ch 34: 'Woe to the shepherds of Israel! They did not feed my flock. I myself will seek my sheep. My servant David will be the shepherd.'

Ch 36: 'Prophesy to the mountains of Israel: I will make you inhabited again. I will vindicate my name. I will put my Spirit within you.'

Ch 37: The Lord said: 'Prophesy to the bones.' The bones became an army. The Lord said: 'Join two sticks. I will join Ephraim and Judah.'

Ch 40: In visions the Lord brought me to the Temple. He brought me through the gates to the inner court. There were tables for offerings.

Ch 43: The glory of the Lord filled the Temple. He said: 'Son of man, describe the Temple to Israel. The priests shall cleanse the altar.'

Something to take away

Sometimes it seems as if all hope has died, but resurrection is God's speciality. He can breathe life even into dry bones.

Daniel

What to expect
The story of four friends who are faithful to God during the exile in Babylon. The book also contains some of Daniel's prophecies.

Chapters 12

Key people
Daniel, Shadrach, Meshach, Abednego, Nebuchadnezzar, Darius.

Timeline

THE BEGINNING · THE PATRIARCHS IN EGYPT · THE WILDERNESS · PROMISED LAND · THE JUDGES · UNITED KINGDOM · DIVIDED KINGDOM · **EXILE IN BABYLON** · RETURN FROM EXILE · LIFE OF JESUS · THE EARLY CHURCH · THE END

Key passage
Daniel 3:14–18

And Nebuchadnezzar said to them, 'Shadrach, Meshach and Abednego, is it true that you don't worship my gods? And is it true that you didn't bow down and worship the gold idol I have set up? Now when you hear the ... musical instruments, you must bow down and worship the gold idol. If you are ready to worship the idol I have made, that is good. But if you don't worship it, you will be thrown ... into the hot furnace. Then no god will be able to save you from my power!'

Shadrach, Meshach and Abednego answered the king, 'Nebuchadnezzar, we don't need to explain these things to you. If you throw us into the hot furnace, the God we serve can save us ... But even if God does not save us, we want you to know, king, that we refuse to serve your gods. We will not worship the gold idol you have set up.'

Chapter summaries (*@BibleSummary*)

Ch 1: Nebuchadnezzar brought the young nobles to Babylon. Daniel resolved not to defile himself with the king's food. God gave him wisdom.

Ch 3: Shadrach, Meshach and Abednego would not worship the gold statue. Nebuchadnezzar threw them into the furnace but God protected them.

Ch 6: The satraps urged Darius to sign a law against prayer. Daniel prayed to God and was thrown to the lions. God closed the lions' mouths.

Ch 7: Daniel saw visions: I saw four great beasts. The Son of Man was given an everlasting kingdom. The fourth beast shall be destroyed.

Ch 9: I read the book of Jeremiah. I prayed, 'Israel has sinned. O God, forgive.' Gabriel said, 'Seventy weeks are decreed for atonement.'

Ch 12: 'There will be a time of distress.' I said, 'How long?' He said, 'Time, times and half a time. These words are sealed until the end.'

Something to take away

We can trust God even when it makes us unpopular. He is directing the big picture of history.

Hosea

What to expect

The first of the shorter books of prophecy. God tells Hosea to marry an unfaithful woman to show that even though Israel has been faithless, God will be faithful.

Chapters 14

Key people
Hosea, Gomer (his unfaithful wife).

Timeline

Key passage
Hosea 3:1

Then the LORD said to me again, 'Your wife has many lovers. But you must continue to love her, because it is an example of the LORD's love for Israel. He continues to love them, but they continue to turn to other gods, and they love to share in the offering of raisin cakes to them.'

Chapter summaries (*@BibleSummary*)

Ch 1: The Lord told Hosea, 'Marry an adulterer for the land has prostituted itself.' Gomer had sons. The Lord said, 'You are not my people.'

Ch 3: The Lord said to me, 'Go, love your wife again as the Lord loves Israel.' So I bought her back. For Israel will return to the Lord.

Ch 4: The Lord has a charge against Israel: 'There is no faithfulness. They have left God to play the whore. The rulers love shameful ways.'

Ch 9: Rejoice not, O Israel! The days of punishment have come. 'I will bereave them. I will drive them from my house.' God will reject them.

Ch 11: 'When Israel was a child, I loved him. But the sword shall devour him. How can I give you up, O Ephraim? I will bring you home.'

Ch 14: O Israel, return to the Lord. 'I will heal their apostasy. They shall blossom like the vine. Whoever is wise, let him understand.'

Something to take away

Many times we chase other things instead of God. Everything else leaves us empty, but God still loves and welcomes us when we turn back to him.

Joel

What to expect
A book of prophecy, foretelling the terrifying day of the Lord's judgement.

Chapters 3

Key people
Joel.

Timeline

Key passage
Joel 1:4

What the cutting locust has left,
*   the swarming locust has eaten.*
And what the swarming locust has left,
*   the hopping locust has eaten.*
And what the hopping locust has left,
*   the destroying locust has eaten!*

Chapter summaries (*@BibleSummary*)

Ch 1: What the locust swarm has left other locusts have eaten. The fields are destroyed. Lament, O priests! The day of the Lord is near.

Ch 2: A great army is on the mountains. Return to the Lord for he is merciful. 'Fear not, I will restore you. I will pour out my Spirit.'

Ch 3: 'I will gather all the nations for judgement. For the day of the Lord is near. Jerusalem will be inhabited for all generations.'

Something to take away

God's judgement is part of his bigger plan to save the world. There is always hope.

Amos

What to expect
A book of prophecy, telling of the
Lord's judgement against Israel.

Chapters 9

Key people
Amos.

Timeline

THE BEGINNING
THE PATRIARCHS
IN EGYPT
THE WILDERNESS
PROMISED LAND
THE JUDGES
UNITED KINGDOM
DIVIDED KINGDOM
EXILE IN BABYLON
RETURN FROM EXILE
LIFE OF JESUS
THE EARLY CHURCH
THE END

Key passage
Amos 5:21–24

'I hate your festivals;
    I will not accept them.
    I don't enjoy your religious meetings.
Even if you offer me burnt offerings and grain offerings,
    I will not accept them.
I will not even look at the fat animals
    you give as fellowship offerings.
Take your noisy songs away from here.
    I will not listen to the music from your harps.
But let justice flow like a river,
    and let goodness flow like a stream that never becomes dry.'

Chapter summaries (*@BibleSummary*)

Ch 1: The Lord says: 'I will punish Damascus. The remnant of the Philistines shall perish. I will send fire upon Tyre, Edom and Ammon.'

Ch 3: Does a lion roar when it has no prey? The Lord reveals his plans to the prophets. 'On the day I punish Israel, I will punish Bethel.'

Ch 5: 'Fallen is virgin Israel. Seek me and live. You shall not dwell in your houses. I despise your feasts. Let justice roll like waters.'

Ch 9: The Lord said: 'Strike the pillars until the earth shakes. I will shake the house of Israel. In that day I will restore my people.'

Something to take away

We can't rely on our religiousness. God is not impressed. He cares about the state of our hearts, and about how we treat the poor.

Obadiah

What to expect
A single chapter of prophecy against Edom, who did nothing when Israel was invaded.

> **Chapters** 1
>
> **Key people**
> Obadiah.

Timeline

Key passage
Obadiah 11,12

You joined the enemies of Israel.
*   Strangers carried Israel's treasures away.*
Foreigners entered Israel's city gate.
*   They threw lots to decide what part of Jerusalem they would get.*
*   And you were right there with them, waiting to get your share.*
You should not have laughed
*   at your brother's trouble.*
You should not have been happy
*   when they destroyed Judah.*
You should not have boasted
*   at the time of their trouble.*

Chapter summaries (*@BibleSummary*)

Ch 1:   The Lord says of Edom: 'What disaster awaits you! You stood
aloof when strangers entered Jerusalem. Saviours shall rule
Mount Esau.'

Something to take away

We can't just stand by and watch when our neighbours are in trouble.
Loving our neighbour is one of God's highest commands.

Jonah

What to expect

The famous story of Jonah's misadventures as he tries to avoid preaching in Nineveh, and then pronounces God's judgement.

Chapters 4

Key people
Jonah; a large fish.

Timeline

THE BEGINNING · THE PATRIARCHS · IN EGYPT · THE WILDERNESS · PROMISED LAND · THE JUDGES · UNITED KINGDOM · **DIVIDED KINGDOM** · EXILE IN BABYLON · RETURN FROM EXILE · LIFE OF JESUS · THE EARLY CHURCH · THE END

Key passage
Jonah 1:10–12

Jonah told the men he was running away from the LORD. The men became very afraid when they learned this. They asked Jonah, 'What terrible thing did you do against your God?'
The wind and the waves of the sea were becoming stronger and stronger. So the men said to Jonah, 'What should we do to save ourselves? What should we do to you to make the sea calm?'
Jonah said to the men, 'I know I did wrong – that is why the storm came on the sea. So throw me into the sea, and the sea will become calm.'

Chapter summaries (*@BibleSummary*)

Ch 1: The Lord sent Jonah to Nineveh. Jonah fled by ship. A storm arose and the men threw Jonah into the sea. A great fish swallowed him.

Ch 2: Jonah prayed: 'I cried out in my distress. Waters surrounded me. You brought me up from the pit!' The fish vomited him onto dry land.

Ch 3: So Jonah went to Nineveh and said, 'Nineveh shall be overthrown!' The people fasted and wore sackcloth. God relented of the disaster.

Ch 4: Jonah was angry and said, 'O Lord, take my life.' A plant sheltered Jonah but it died. The Lord said, 'Should I not pity Nineveh?'

Something to take away

There's no sense in running away from God. You can't escape him even if you sail across the ocean. He will challenge you and guide you back onto the right path.

Micah

What to expect

A book of prophecy, reassuring Israel that even though disaster has come, God will send a saviour.

Chapters 7

Key people
Micah.

Timeline

Key passage
Micah 5:3,4

The LORD will let his people be defeated
  until the woman gives birth to her child, the promised king.
Then the rest of his brothers will come back
  to join the people of Israel.
He will begin to rule Israel in the power of the LORD.
  Like a shepherd, he will lead his people in the wonderful name of the
    LORD his God.
And they will live in safety
  because then his greatness will be known all over the world.

Chapter summaries (*@BibleSummary*)

Ch 1: The Lord is coming! The mountains will melt. 'I will make Samaria a ruin.' Her wound is incurable. Disaster has come to Jerusalem.

Ch 4: In the last days, nations will come to the mountain of the Lord. Zion will be rescued from Babylon. 'I will give you horns of iron.'

Ch 5: 'From you, O Bethlehem, will come a ruler.' The remnant of Jacob will be like a lion. 'I will punish the nations that did not obey.'

Ch 6: 'O my people, have I wearied you?' What does the Lord require? Act justly and love mercy. 'I will make you desolate for your sins.'

Ch 7: The godly have perished from the earth. But I will look to the Lord. The nations will tremble. Who is a God like you, forgiving sin?

Something to take away
Even when God judges sin, he is working for our salvation. We can see that mostly clearly when Jesus is punished for sins on the cross and wins our salvation.

Nahum

What to expect
A prophecy against the Assyrian city of Nineveh. Assyria had often attacked the Israelites.

Chapters 3

Key people
Nahum.

Timeline

THE BEGINNING · THE PATRIARCHS · IN EGYPT · THE WILDERNESS · PROMISED LAND · THE JUDGES · UNITED KINGDOM · **DIVIDED KINGDOM** · EXILE IN BABYLON · RETURN FROM EXILE · LIFE OF JESUS · THE EARLY CHURCH · THE END

Key passage
Nahum 2:13

The Lord All-Powerful says,
  'I am against you, Nineveh.
I will burn your chariots
  and kill your "young lions" in battle.
  You will not hunt anyone on earth again.
People will never again hear bad news
  from your messengers.'

Chapter summaries (*@BibleSummary*)

Ch 1: Against Nineveh: The Lord takes vengeance on his enemies. The Lord says, 'I will break his yoke from you.' Hold your feasts, O Judah!

Ch 2: The Lord is restoring Jacob. Chariots race through the streets. Nineveh is like a draining pool. 'I am against you,' declares the Lord.

Ch 3: Woe to the bloody city! 'The nations will look at your shame.' Draw water for the siege. Your shepherds are asleep, O king of Assyria.

Something to take away

Evil and injustice will not go unpunished. In the end everything will be made right.

Habakkuk

What to expect
A prayer of complaint by the prophet Habakkuk, questioning why God would use the Babylonians to punish Judah.

Chapters 3

Key people
Habakkuk.

Timeline

THE BEGINNING · THE PATRIARCHS · IN EGYPT · THE WILDERNESS · PROMISED LAND · THE JUDGES · UNITED KINGDOM · **DIVIDED KINGDOM** · **EXILE IN BABYLON** · RETURN FROM EXILE · LIFE OF JESUS · THE EARLY CHURCH · THE END

Key passage
Habakkuk 3:2

LORD, I have heard the news about you.
    I am amazed, LORD, at the powerful things you did in the past.
Now I pray that you will do great things in our time.
    Please make these things happen in our own days.
But in your anger,
    remember to show mercy to us.

Chapter summaries (*@BibleSummary*)

Ch 1: O Lord, why do you tolerate evil? 'Behold, I am raising up the Chaldeans.' Your eyes are pure. Why do you look upon the treacherous?

Ch 2: The Lord answered: 'The just shall live by faith. Woe to him who plunders nations! What profit is an idol? The Lord is in his Temple.'

Ch 3: O Lord, renew your works! He stood and shook the earth. You crushed the head of the wicked. I will rejoice in the God of my salvation.

Something to take away
Even though God is able to turn evil actions into greater good, those who have done evil will still be judged.

Zephaniah

What to expect
A prophecy about the vengeance of God.

Chapters 3

Key people
Zephaniah.

Timeline

Key passage
Zephaniah 1:14–16

The Lord's special day for judging is coming soon! It is near and coming fast. People will hear very sad sounds on the Lord's special day of judgement. Even strong soldiers will cry. The Lord will show his anger at that time. It will be a time of terrible troubles and a time of destruction. It will be a time of darkness – a black, cloudy and stormy day. It will be like a time of war when people hear horns and trumpets in the defence towers and protected cities.

Chapter summaries (*@BibleSummary*)

Ch 1: 'I will sweep away everything from the earth,' declares the Lord. The day of the Lord is near. 'I will bring distress on mankind.'

Ch 2: Seek the Lord, you humble. Gaza shall be deserted. The Lord is against you, O Canaan. He will stretch out his hand to destroy Assyria.

Ch 3: Woe to the rebellious city! 'I have cut off nations. I will leave a humble people.' Sing, O Zion! The Lord will quiet you by his love.

Something to take away

God will be the judge of everything. Even as he judges those who have done evil, he will bring peace to his people.

Haggai

What to expect
A book of prophecy encouraging the people of Israel to rebuild the Temple after they returned from exile in Babylon.

Chapters 2

Key people
Haggai, Zerubbabel.

Timeline

THE BEGINNING · THE PATRIARCHS · IN EGYPT · THE WILDERNESS · PROMISED LAND · THE JUDGES · UNITED KINGDOM · DIVIDED KINGDOM · EXILE IN BABYLON · **RETURN FROM EXILE** · LIFE OF JESUS · THE EARLY CHURCH · THE END

Key passage
Haggai 1:7–8

The Lᴏʀᴅ All-Powerful said, 'Think about what you are doing. Go up to the mountains, get the wood, and build the Temple. Then I will be pleased with the Temple, and I will be honoured.' This is what the Lᴏʀᴅ said.

Haggai

Chapter summaries (*@BibleSummary*)

Ch 1: The Lord says: 'Consider your ways! You never have enough because the Temple lies in ruins.' So the people worked on the Temple.

Ch 2: The Lord says: 'The latter glory of this Temple shall be greater than the former. This nation is unclean. But now I will bless you.'

Something to take away

How can anything else go right if our worship lives are not in order? For our own good we should prioritize worship.

Zechariah

What to expect
Prophecies about the Lord's day of judgement and his promised saviour. Many of Zechariah's prophecies foreshadow events in Jesus' life.

Chapters 14

Key people
Zechariah, Joshua the high priest.

Timeline

THE BEGINNING
THE PATRIARCHS
IN EGYPT
THE WILDERNESS
PROMISED LAND
THE JUDGES
UNITED KINGDOM
DIVIDED KINGDOM
EXILE IN BABYLON
RETURN FROM EXILE
LIFE OF JESUS
THE EARLY CHURCH
THE END

Key passage
Zechariah 9:9

People of Zion, rejoice!
*   *People of Jerusalem, shout with joy!*
Look, your king is coming to you!
*   *He is the good king who won the victory, but he is humble.*
*   *He is riding on a donkey, on a young donkey born from a work animal.*

Chapter summaries (*@BibleSummary*)

Ch 1: The Lord said, 'Return to me.' So the people repented. I saw a man on a red horse. The Lord said, 'I will return to Zion with mercy.'

Ch 4: I saw a lampstand. I asked the angel about it. 'Not by might but by my Spirit,' says the Lord. 'Zerubbabel will complete the Temple.'

Ch 6: I saw four chariots with red, black, white and dappled horses. The Lord said, 'Make a crown for Joshua. He shall build the Temple.'

Ch 7: The people asked, 'Should we fast?' The Lord said, 'Show mercy and do not oppress. But they would not listen. So I scattered them.'

Ch 10: Ask the Lord for rain. From Judah will come the cornerstone. 'I will save Judah for I am the Lord their God. I will bring them home.'

Ch 13: 'There will be a fountain to cleanse from sin. I will remove prophets from the land. Strike my shepherd and the sheep will scatter.'

Ch 14: A day is coming when the Lord will go into battle. Jerusalem will dwell in security. All the nations will worship the Lord of hosts.

Something to take away

All God's ways point to Jesus, and Jesus shows us what God is like in all his ways.

Malachi

What to expect
Another prophecy about the Lord's day of judgement. He will send a new Elijah ahead to announce his judgement and salvation.

Chapters 4

Key people
Malachi.

Timeline

THE BEGINNING · THE PATRIARCHS · IN EGYPT · THE WILDERNESS · PROMISED LAND · THE JUDGES · UNITED KINGDOM · DIVIDED KINGDOM · EXILE IN BABYLON · RETURN FROM EXILE · LIFE OF JESUS · THE EARLY CHURCH · THE END

Key passage
Malachi 3:1

The Lord All-Powerful says, 'I am sending my messenger to prepare the way for me. Then suddenly, the Lord you are looking for will come to his temple. Yes, the messenger you are waiting for, the one who will tell about my agreement, is really coming!'

Chapter summaries (@*BibleSummary*)

Ch 1: 'I have loved you,' says the Lord. 'Where is my honour? You offer blind and lame sacrifices. My name will be great among the nations.'

Ch 3: 'My messenger will prepare the way. I will come to judge. You have robbed me of tithes. The Lord will remember those who serve him.'

Ch 4: 'The day is coming like a furnace. The sun of righteousness will rise. The wicked will be ashes. I will send you Elijah the prophet.'

Something to take away

God deserves our best. If we try to give him less, we may find that he challenges and judges our half-heartedness.

THE NEW TESTAMENT

What to expect

The story of Jesus and the church. God sends his Son to save the world. Jesus teaches, performs miracles and calls disciples. He is crucified and rises again. His followers tell everyone the good news and start churches.

Books

27

Sections

The Gospels – Matthew, Mark, Luke, John

The Story of the Early Church – Acts

Letters from Paul – Romans, 1 & 2 Corinthians, Galatians, Ephesians, Philippians, Colossians, 1 & 2 Thessalonians, 1 & 2 Timothy, Titus, Philemon

Other Letters – Hebrews, James, 1 & 2 Peter, 1, 2 & 3 John, Jude

The End – Revelation

Timeline

THE BEGINNING · THE PATRIARCHS · IN EGYPT · THE WILDERNESS · PROMISED LAND · THE JUDGES · UNITED KINGDOM · DIVIDED KINGDOM · EXILE IN BABYLON · RETURN FROM EXILE · **LIFE OF JESUS · THE EARLY CHURCH · THE END**

Matthew

What to expect

The story of Jesus' birth, miracles, teaching, death and resurrection. Matthew's gospel is structured around five of Jesus' sermons.

Chapters 28

Key people
Jesus, the twelve disciples.

Timeline

THE BEGINNING · THE PATRIARCHS · IN EGYPT · THE WILDERNESS · PROMISED LAND · THE JUDGES · UNITED KINGDOM · DIVIDED KINGDOM · EXILE IN BABYLON · RETURN FROM EXILE · LIFE OF JESUS · THE EARLY CHURCH · THE END

Key passage
Matthew 5:17–20

'Don't think that I have come to destroy the Law of Moses or the teaching of the prophets. I have come not to destroy their teachings but to give full meaning to them. I assure you that nothing will disappear from the law until heaven and earth are gone. The law will not lose even the smallest letter or the smallest part of a letter until it has all been done.
'A person should obey every command in the law, even one that does not seem important. Whoever refuses to obey any command and teaches others not to obey it will be the least important in God's kingdom. But whoever obeys the law and teaches others to obey it will be great in God's kingdom. I tell you that you must do better than the teachers of the law and the Pharisees. If you are not more pleasing to God than they are, you will never enter God's kingdom.'

Chapter summaries (@BibleSummary)

Ch 1: The record of Jesus Christ, son of David, son of Abraham. Mary bore a son by the Holy Spirit. An angel told Joseph to name him Jesus.

Ch 3: John the Baptist was preaching, 'Repent, the kingdom is near!' Jesus was baptized by John. A voice from heaven said, 'This is my Son.'

Ch 4: Jesus was tempted by Satan in the wilderness. He called Peter, Andrew, James and John to follow him. He preached and healed the sick.

Ch 5: Jesus said, 'Blessed are the pure in heart. I have come to fulfil the law. Whoever is angry will be judged. I say, love your enemies.'

Ch 8: Jesus healed a man with leprosy. He healed the servant of a centurion who had faith. He calmed a storm and cast demons out of two men.

Ch 10: Jesus sent out the twelve to proclaim the kingdom. 'You will be hated for my name, but do not fear. Whoever receives you receives me.'

Ch 13: Jesus gave a parable about a sower. He told the disciples, 'Seeing they do not see.' He said, 'The kingdom is like hidden treasure.'

Ch 16: Peter said, 'You are the Christ.' Jesus told them that he must be killed and be raised. He said, 'Take up your cross and follow me.'

Ch 21: Jesus rode into Jerusalem on a donkey. He healed and taught in the Temple. 'A man sent his son to his tenants, but they killed him.'

Matthew

Ch 23: Jesus said, 'The Pharisees preach but do not practise. You strain out a gnat but swallow a camel. You kill and crucify the prophets.'

Ch 26: Jesus took Passover with his disciples. He prayed in agony in Gethsemane. Judas betrayed Jesus to the chief priests. Peter denied him.

Ch 27: Jesus was handed over to Pilate. The crowd said, 'Crucify him!' He was mocked and crucified. Darkness fell and he gave up his spirit.

Ch 28: The women went to the tomb. An angel said, 'He has risen!' Jesus met them. He came to the eleven and said, 'Go and make disciples.'

Something to take away

Jesus had authority from God in his teaching and in his actions. He has given us that same authority.

Mark

What to expect
The shortest gospel. The first half tells the story of Jesus' miracles and teaching, the second half tells the story of Jesus' death and resurrection.

Chapters 16

Key people
Jesus, the twelve disciples.

Timeline

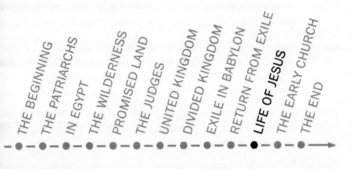

THE BEGINNING · THE PATRIARCHS · IN EGYPT · THE WILDERNESS · PROMISED LAND · THE JUDGES · UNITED KINGDOM · DIVIDED KINGDOM · EXILE IN BABYLON · RETURN FROM EXILE · LIFE OF JESUS · THE EARLY CHURCH · THE END

Key passage
Mark 3:1–6

Another time Jesus went into the synagogue. In the synagogue there was a man with a paralysed hand. Some Jews there were watching Jesus closely. They were waiting to see if he would heal the man on a Sabbath day. They wanted to see Jesus do something wrong so that they could accuse him. Jesus said to the man with the paralysed hand, 'Stand up here so that everyone can see you.'
Then Jesus asked the people, 'Which is the right thing to do on the Sabbath day: to do good or to do evil? Is it right to save a life or to destroy one?' The people said nothing to answer him.
Jesus looked at the people. He was angry, but he felt very sad because they were so stubborn. He said to the man, 'Hold out your hand.' The man held out his hand, and it was healed. Then the Pharisees left and made plans with the Herodians about a way to kill Jesus.

Mark

Chapter summaries (*@BibleSummary*)

Ch 1: Jesus was baptized by John. He called Simon, Andrew, James and John. He preached and cast out demons. He healed a man with leprosy.

Ch 3: Jesus healed a man on the Sabbath. Great crowds followed him. He appointed twelve apostles. He said, 'Whoever obeys God is my family.'

Ch 6: He sent the twelve out to preach. Herod executed John the Baptist. Jesus fed 5,000 men. He came to the disciples walking on the sea.

Ch 8: Jesus fed 4,000 people and healed a blind man. Peter said, 'You are the Christ.' Jesus told them that he must be killed and rise again.

Ch 9: Jesus took Peter, James and John and was transfigured. He healed a boy with seizures. The disciples argued which of them was greatest.

Ch 11: Jesus rode into Jerusalem on a donkey. He drove the money-changers from the Temple. The elders asked, 'Who gave you this authority?'

Ch 14: Jesus took Passover with his disciples. He prayed in agony in Gethsemane. Judas betrayed him to the chief priests. Peter denied him.

Ch 15: Jesus was handed over to Pilate. The crowd cried, 'Crucify him!' He was mocked and crucified. Darkness fell and he breathed his last.

Ch 16: The women went to the tomb. A man in white said, 'He has risen!' Jesus appeared to the disciples. He said, 'Go and preach the gospel.'

Something to take away

Jesus knew exactly when to challenge people and when to comfort them. Do you need to hear a challenge or do you need to be comforted?

Luke

What to expect

The story of Jesus' birth, miracles, teaching, death and resurrection. Luke tells lots of unique stories from Jesus' final journey to Jerusalem.

Chapters 24

Key people

Jesus, the twelve disciples.

Timeline

THE BEGINNING · THE PATRIARCHS · IN EGYPT · THE WILDERNESS · PROMISED LAND · THE JUDGES · UNITED KINGDOM · DIVIDED KINGDOM · EXILE IN BABYLON · RETURN FROM EXILE · LIFE OF JESUS · THE EARLY CHURCH · THE END

Key passage
Luke 23:32–34a

There were also two criminals led out with Jesus to be killed. They were led to a place called 'The Skull'. There the soldiers nailed Jesus to the cross. They also nailed the criminals to crosses beside Jesus – one on the right and the other on the left.
And Jesus was saying, 'Father, forgive these people, because they do not know what they are doing.'

Luke

Chapter summaries (*@BibleSummary*)

Ch 1: The angel Gabriel foretold the birth of John. He told Mary, 'You will have a son named Jesus.' Mary said, 'My soul magnifies the Lord!'

Ch 3: John came from the wilderness preaching repentance. Jesus was baptized. He was son of David, son of Abraham, son of Adam, son of God.

Ch 4: Jesus was tempted by Satan in the wilderness. In the synagogue he read out, 'The Spirit of the Lord is on me.' He healed all the sick.

Ch 6: Jesus healed a man on the Sabbath. He chose twelve apostles. He said, 'Blessed are the poor. Love your enemies. Hear and do my words.'

Ch 9: Jesus sent out the twelve. He fed 5,000 men. Peter said, 'You are the Christ.' Jesus said, 'Take up your cross.' He was transfigured.

Ch 15: Jesus said, 'Heaven rejoices when a sinner repents. A son squandered his father's wealth. He returned and his father called a feast.'

Ch 17: Jesus said, 'If your brother repents, forgive him.' He healed ten men with leprosy. 'In his day the Son of Man will light up the sky.'

Ch 19: Jesus ate with Zacchaeus. He told a parable about servants in the kingdom. He rode into Jerusalem on a colt and wept over the city.

Ch 21: Jesus said, 'The Temple will be thrown down. Jerusalem will be trampled. The Son of Man will come in glory. Stay awake at all times.'

Ch 22: Jesus took Passover with the disciples. He prayed at the Mount of Olives. Judas betrayed him to the chief priests. Peter denied him.

Ch 23: Jesus was taken to Pilate. The crowd said, 'Crucify him!' He was crucified with two criminals. Darkness fell and he breathed his last.

Ch 24: The women found the tomb empty. Jesus met two on the road to Emmaus. He appeared to the disciples and opened the Scriptures to them.

Something to take away

Jesus was totally clear that his mission would lead him to die for the sins of the world. Are we living for the kingdom whatever the cost?

John

What to expect

The story of Jesus' ministry,
teaching, death and resurrection.
John tells lots of stories that aren't
included in the other three gospels.
He emphasizes that Jesus is God
himself.

Chapters 21

Key people
Jesus, the twelve disciples.

Timeline

Key passage
John 1:1–5

*Before the world began, the Word was there. The Word was with God, and
the Word was God. He was there with God in the beginning. Everything
was made through him, and nothing was made without him. In him there
was life, and that life was a light for the people of the world. The light
shines in the darkness, and the darkness has not defeated it.*

Chapter summaries (@*BibleSummary*)

Ch 1: The Word of God became flesh and dwelt with us. John the Baptist bore witness to him. Andrew told Simon Peter and they followed Jesus.

Ch 3: Jesus told Nicodemus, 'Be born again. Whoever believes in the Son will have eternal life.' John the Baptist said, 'He is above all.'

Ch 5: Jesus healed a man at Bethesda. He said, 'The Son only does what he sees the Father doing. My works and the Scriptures bear witness.'

Ch 6: Jesus fed 5,000 men and walked across the sea. He said, 'I am the bread of life. My flesh is true food.' Many disciples turned back.

Ch 7: Jesus went to the feast. The people said, 'Is this the Christ?' The chief priests tried to arrest him. He called out, 'Come and drink.'

Ch 10: Jesus said, 'I am the good shepherd. I give my life for the sheep.' They asked, 'Are you the Christ?' He said, 'My sheep follow me.'

Ch 12: Jesus rode into Jerusalem. The crowd shouted, 'Hosanna!' He said, 'The Son of Man must be lifted up. I have come to save the world.'

Ch 13: Jesus washed the disciples' feet. He said, 'One of you will betray me.' Judas left. Jesus said, 'Love each other as I have loved you.'

Ch 14: 'I am the way, the truth, and the life. I am in the Father and the Father in me. He will give you the Holy Spirit. Do not be afraid.'

Ch 18: Judas betrayed Jesus to the chief priests. Peter denied him. He was sent before Pilate. Jesus said, 'My kingdom is not of this world.'

John

Ch 19: The soldiers took Jesus and crucified him. He said, 'It is finished.' He gave up his spirit. A soldier pierced his side with a spear.

Ch 20: Mary went to the tomb and found it empty. Jesus met her. He came and stood among the disciples. Thomas said, 'My Lord and my God!'

Something to take away

Jesus wasn't just a good teacher, he was God himself living amongst us. He now lives *in* us by the Holy Spirit. Have you thought about how revolutionary a claim that is?

Acts

What to expect

Luke picks up the story after Jesus' resurrection. The Spirit comes at Pentecost, Paul is converted on the road to Damascus, and many new churches are established.

Chapters 28

Key people
Peter, Paul (also called Saul), Barnabas, the early churches.

Timeline

THE BEGINNING
THE PATRIARCHS
IN EGYPT
THE WILDERNESS
PROMISED LAND
THE JUDGES
UNITED KINGDOM
DIVIDED KINGDOM
EXILE IN BABYLON
RETURN FROM EXILE
LIFE OF JESUS
THE EARLY CHURCH
THE END

Key passage
Acts 2:38–41

Peter said to them, 'Change your hearts and lives and be baptized, each one of you, in the name of Jesus Christ. Then God will forgive your sins, and you will receive the gift of the Holy Spirit. This promise is for you. It is also for your children and for the people who are far away. It is for everyone the Lord our God calls to himself.'
Peter warned them with many other words; he begged them, 'Save yourselves from the evil of the people who live now!' Then those who accepted what Peter said were baptized. On that day about 3,000 people were added to the group of believers.

Acts

Chapter summaries (*@BibleSummary*)

Ch 2:   At Pentecost they were filled with the Spirit. Peter told the crowd, 'You crucified Jesus but God has made him Lord.' 3,000 believed.

Ch 3:   Peter and John healed a lame man at the Temple. Peter told the people, 'Faith in Jesus has healed this man. Repent of your sins.'

Ch 4:   They were taken before the rulers. Peter and John said, 'We cannot stop speaking about Jesus.' The believers prayed for boldness.

Ch 9:   Saul went to arrest the believers. Jesus said, 'Why do you persecute me?' Saul was baptized and began preaching. Peter raised Dorcas.

Ch 10:   Cornelius sent for Peter. The Lord said to Peter, 'Do not call them unclean.' Peter preached to the Gentiles and the Spirit came.

Ch 13:   Paul and Barnabas proclaimed the word. Paul said, 'God has sent a Saviour, Jesus, as he promised.' The Jews stirred up persecution.

Ch 15:   Some men taught circumcision for the Gentiles. Peter said, 'God gave the Spirit with no distinction.' Paul and Barnabas separated.

Ch 18:   Paul taught in Corinth for a year and a half. He went to Ephesus with Priscilla and Aquila. Priscilla and Aquila taught Apollos.

Ch 21:   Paul was warned not to go to Jerusalem. He said, 'I am ready to die.' We went there and saw James. Paul was arrested in the Temple.

Ch 23: Paul caused a dispute between the Pharisees and Sadducees. The Jews plotted to kill him. The tribune sent him to Governor Felix.

Ch 25: Festus arrived and summoned Paul. Paul said, 'I appeal to Caesar.' Festus brought Paul before king Agrippa to decide the charges.

Ch 27: They set sail for Rome. A storm struck and all hope was lost. Paul said, 'Take heart, we must run aground.' Everyone reached land.

Ch 28: On Malta Paul healed all who had diseases. He came to Rome. Paul lived under house arrest. He proclaimed the kingdom of God to all.

Something to take away
The Holy Spirit gave the early church power to carry on Jesus' mission. That same power is available for us today!

Romans

What to expect
A letter from Paul to the church in Rome. He explains the gospel, comparing life under the Old Testament law with new life in Christ.

Chapters 16

Key people
Paul, the church in Rome.

Timeline

THE BEGINNING · THE PATRIARCHS · IN EGYPT · THE WILDERNESS · PROMISED LAND · THE JUDGES · UNITED KINGDOM · DIVIDED KINGDOM · EXILE IN BABYLON · RETURN FROM EXILE · LIFE OF JESUS · **THE EARLY CHURCH** · THE END

Key passage
Romans 8:1–4

So now anyone who is in Christ Jesus is not judged guilty. That is because in Christ Jesus the law of the Spirit that brings life made you free. It made you free from the law that brings sin and death. The law was without power because it was made weak by our sinful selves. But God did what the law could not do: he sent his own Son to earth with the same human life that everyone else uses for sin. God sent him to be an offering to pay for sin. So God used a human life to destroy sin. He did this so that we could be right just as the law said we must be. Now we don't live following our sinful selves. We live following the Spirit.

Chapter summaries (@BibleSummary)

Ch 1: Paul, to the saints in Rome. I am eager to preach the gospel to you. The unrighteous have no excuse. God gave them up to their lusts.

Ch 2: In judging you condemn yourself. The doers of the law will be justified. Do you boast in the law but break it? A Jew is one inwardly.

Ch 3: The Jews were given the oracles of God. But no one is justified by the law. All have sinned and are justified through faith in Jesus.

Ch 6: We were baptized into Christ's death. So consider yourselves dead to sin and alive to God. Offer yourselves to God for righteousness.

Ch 7: You have died to the law. Is the law sin? No, sin produced death in me. I do not do what I want to do. My flesh serves the law of sin.

Ch 8: The law of the Spirit has set you free. We are children of God and co-heirs with Christ. Nothing can separate us from the love of God.

Ch 9: I grieve for my kinsmen. But not all Israel are Israel. God has mercy on whom he wills. Israel did not pursue righteousness by faith.

Ch 11: Even now there is a remnant of Israel. You Gentiles have been grafted into the tree. All Israel will be saved. Glory to God for ever!

Ch 12: Present your bodies as a living sacrifice to God. We are one body in Christ. Love one another as brothers. Overcome evil with good.

Something to take away

We were all dead in sin, but God has completely saved us in Christ. We only have to hope in him.

1 Corinthians

What to expect

A letter to the church in Corinth. Paul answers questions about lots of practical issues, including ministry, sex, spiritual gifts and resurrection.

Chapters 16

Key people
Paul, the church in Corinth.

Timeline

THE BEGINNING · THE PATRIARCHS · IN EGYPT · THE WILDERNESS · PROMISED LAND · THE JUDGES · UNITED KINGDOM · DIVIDED KINGDOM · EXILE IN BABYLON · RETURN FROM EXILE · LIFE OF JESUS · **THE EARLY CHURCH** · THE END

Key passage
1 Corinthians 8:9–12

But be careful with your freedom. Your freedom to eat anything may make those who have doubts about what they can eat fall into sin. You understand that it's all right to eat anything, so you can eat even in an idol's temple. But someone who has doubts might see you eating there, and this might encourage them to eat meat sacrificed to idols too. But they really think it is wrong. So this weak brother or sister – someone Christ died for – is lost because of your better understanding. When you sin against your brothers and sisters in Christ in this way and you hurt them by causing them to do things they feel are wrong, you are also sinning against Christ.

Chapter summaries (*@BibleSummary*)

Ch 1: Paul, to the church in Corinth. Let there be no divisions. The cross is folly to those perishing, but to us it is the power of God.

Ch 3: You are still infants. One follows Paul, another Apollos. We are co-workers with God. Christ is the foundation. You are God's temple.

Ch 6: Do you take one another to court? Why not rather be wronged? Your body is not for sexual immorality, it is a temple of the Spirit.

Ch 9: You are the seal of my apostleship. Do we not have the right to material support? But I made myself a servant to all for the gospel.

Ch 12: Now there are various spiritual gifts, but one Spirit. If the whole body were an eye, how would it hear? You are the body of Christ.

Ch 13: Without love I am nothing. Love is patient, does not boast, endures all things. Tongues will cease, but faith, hope and love remain.

Ch 15: Christ was raised from the dead. If not then your faith is futile. But he is the first fruits. At the trumpet we will all be changed.

Something to take away

Churches are always full of imperfect people. We need to rely on God's grace to love and serve one another.

2 Corinthians

What to expect
A follow-up letter from Paul to the church in Corinth. He defends his status as an apostle and talks about his struggles.

Chapters 13

Key people
Paul, the church in Corinth.

Timeline

Key passage
2 Corinthians 4:7–12

We have this treasure from God, but we are only like clay jars that hold the treasure. This is to show that the amazing power we have is from God, not from us. We have troubles all around us, but we are not defeated. We often don't know what to do, but we don't give up. We are persecuted, but God does not leave us. We are hurt sometimes, but we are not destroyed. So we constantly experience the death of Jesus in our own bodies, but this is so that the life of Jesus can also be seen in our bodies. We are alive, but for Jesus we are always in danger of death, so that the life of Jesus can be seen in our bodies that die. So death is working in us, but the result is that life is working in you.

Chapter summaries (*@BibleSummary*)

Ch 1: Paul, to the church in Corinth. We share in Christ's sufferings and comfort. My yes is not no, but to spare you I did not visit you.

Ch 3: God has made us ministers of a new covenant. When anyone turns to the Lord, the veil is lifted. We are being transformed into glory.

Ch 5: What is mortal will be clothed with life. If anyone is in Christ, the new creation has come. We implore you, be reconciled to God!

Ch 7: I take great pride in you. I do not regret my letter, for godly grief produces repentance. Our boasts about you to Titus proved true.

Ch 9: I boast to the Macedonians about the gift you promised. God loves a cheerful giver. Your generosity will overflow in thanksgivings.

Ch 11: I am jealous for you against these false apostles. I speak as a fool. Do they boast? I have greater labours, beatings and dangers.

Ch 12: I will boast of a man who saw paradise. I was given a thorn to keep me from pride. This is foolish! I will gladly be spent for you.

Something to take away

Paul didn't try to use his calling from God for his own advantage. He was content with hardships as well as blessings. Do we have the same attitude?

Galatians

What to expect

An angry letter from Paul to the church in Galatia. He criticizes those who are persuading the Galatians that they should keep the Old Testament law.

Chapters 6

Key people
Paul, the church in Galatia.

Timeline

THE BEGINNING · THE PATRIARCHS · IN EGYPT · THE WILDERNESS · PROMISED LAND · THE JUDGES · UNITED KINGDOM · DIVIDED KINGDOM · EXILE IN BABYLON · RETURN FROM EXILE · LIFE OF JESUS · **THE EARLY CHURCH** · THE END

Key passage
Galatians 3:1–3

You people in Galatia are so foolish! Why do I say this? Because I told you very clearly about the death of Jesus Christ on the cross. But now it seems as though you have let someone use their magical powers to make you forget. Tell me this one thing: how did you receive the Spirit? Did you receive the Spirit by following the law? No, you received the Spirit because you heard the message about Jesus and believed it. You began your life in Christ with the Spirit. Now do you try to complete it by your own power? That is foolish.

Chapter summaries (*@BibleSummary*)

Ch 1: Paul, to the churches of Galatia. You are already turning to a different gospel! The gospel I preached came by revelation from Christ.

Ch 2: I went up to Jerusalem and saw the leaders. I opposed Cephas about circumcision. We are justified by faith in Christ and not by works.

Ch 3: Those who are of faith are blessed with Abraham. Christ has redeemed us from the curse of the law. In Christ you are all sons of God.

Ch 5: Christ has set us free. Circumcision counts for nothing. Use your freedom to love one another. Walk by the Spirit and not the flesh.

Something to take away

Sometimes it seems simpler to follow religious rules and traditions than to depend on Christ, but that's a terrible trade!

Ephesians

What to expect
A letter from Paul to the church in Ephesus. He teaches on unity in the body of Christ and how we should live in the Christian community.

Chapters 6

Key people
Paul, the church in Ephesus.

Timeline

Key passage
Ephesians 4:1–6

So, as a prisoner for the Lord, I beg you to live the way God's people should live, because he chose you to be his. Always be humble and gentle. Be patient and accept each other with love. You are joined together with peace through the Spirit. Do all you can to continue as you are, letting peace hold you together. There is one body and one Spirit, and God chose you to have one hope. There is one Lord, one faith and one baptism. There is one God and Father of us all, who rules over everyone. He works through all of us and in all of us.

Chapter summaries (@*BibleSummary*)

Ch 1: Paul, to the saints in Ephesus. Praise the God who predestined us for adoption in Christ. May you know the riches of his inheritance.

Ch 2: When we were dead in sin God made us alive with Christ. Gentiles are now fellow citizens. You are being built together into a temple.

Ch 3: I preach the mystery of Christ. The wisdom of God is made known through the church. I pray that you may know the depth of his love.

Ch 4: Therefore walk worthy of your calling. Christ gave each of us gifts to build up the body. Put off your old self and put on the new.

Ch 5: Walk in love as Christ loved us. Walk as children of light. Expose the darkness. Husbands, love your wives as Christ loved the church.

Ch 6: Children, obey your parents. Slaves, obey your masters. Put on the whole armour of God to stand against the devil. Peace and grace.

Something to take away

God has put us together in the church to show his incredible plan to save the whole world. Don't let your frustrations give you a smaller vision of what we're called to be together.

Philippians

What to expect
A joyful letter written by Paul from prison to the church in Philippi. He thanks the Philippians for their support for him.

Chapters 4

Key people
Paul, the church in Philippi.

Timeline

THE BEGINNING · THE PATRIARCHS · IN EGYPT · THE WILDERNESS · PROMISED LAND · THE JUDGES · UNITED KINGDOM · DIVIDED KINGDOM · EXILE IN BABYLON · RETURN FROM EXILE · LIFE OF JESUS · **THE EARLY CHURCH** · THE END

Key passage
Philippians 4:10–13

I am so happy, and I thank the Lord that you have again shown your care for me. You continued to care about me, but there was no way for you to show it. I am telling you this, but not because I need something. I have learned to be satisfied with what I have and with whatever happens. I know how to live when I am poor and when I have plenty. I have learned the secret of how to live through any kind of situation – when I have enough to eat or when I am hungry, when I have everything I need or when I have nothing. Christ is the one who gives me the strength I need to do whatever I must do.

Chapter summaries (*@BibleSummary*)

Ch 1: Paul, to the saints in Philippi. I thank God for you. My imprisonment has advanced the gospel. To live is Christ and to die is gain.

Ch 2: Have the mind of Christ, who humbled himself even to a cross. Work out your salvation with trembling. I hope to send Timothy to you.

Ch 3: We put no confidence in the flesh. I count all things as loss compared to Christ. I press on towards the prize. Brothers, imitate me.

Ch 4: Rejoice in the Lord always! The peace of God will guard your hearts. I rejoice at your concern for me. My God will supply your needs.

Something to take away

We have such incredible blessings in Christ. We still have something to celebrate even in the hardest times.

Colossians

What to expect
A letter from Paul to the church in Colossae. He urges them to keep their focus on Christ and not to take on extra religious rules.

Chapters 4

Key people
Paul, the church in Colossae.

Timeline

THE BEGINNING · THE PATRIARCHS · IN EGYPT · THE WILDERNESS · PROMISED LAND · THE JUDGES · UNITED KINGDOM · DIVIDED KINGDOM · EXILE IN BABYLON · RETURN FROM EXILE · LIFE OF JESUS · **THE EARLY CHURCH** · THE END

Key passage
Colossians 3:1–4

You were raised from death with Christ. So live for what is in heaven, where Christ is sitting at the right hand of God. Think only about what is up there, not what is here on earth. Your old self has died, and your new life is kept with Christ in God. Yes, Christ is now your life, and when he comes again, you will share in his glory.

Chapter summaries (*@BibleSummary*)

Ch 1: Paul, to the saints in Colossae. May you be filled with wisdom. The Son is the image of the invisible God. I make known the mystery.

Ch 2: Let no one deceive you. You were buried with Christ and also raised with him. Why do you follow rules that do not restrain the flesh?

Ch 3: Seek the things above. Your life is hidden with Christ in God. So put to death your worldliness. Do everything in the name of Jesus.

Something to take away

we're tempted by worldly things, we only have to fix our eyes on Christ to shift our whole perspective.

1 Thessalonians

What to expect
A letter from Paul and his team to the church in Thessalonica, encouraging the believers to live in the hope of the resurrection.

Chapters 5

Key people
Paul, Timothy, the church in Thessalonica.

Timeline

THE BEGINNING · THE PATRIARCHS · IN EGYPT · THE WILDERNESS · PROMISED LAND · THE JUDGES · UNITED KINGDOM · DIVIDED KINGDOM · EXILE IN BABYLON · RETURN FROM EXILE · LIFE OF JESUS · **THE EARLY CHURCH** · THE END

Key passage
1 Thessalonians 5:2–6

You know very well that the day when the Lord comes again will be a surprise, like a thief who comes at night. People will say, 'We have peace and we are safe.' At that time destruction will come to them quickly, like the pains of a woman giving birth. And those people will not escape. But you, brothers and sisters, are not living in darkness. And so that day will not surprise you like a thief. You are all people who belong to the light. You belong to the day. We don't belong to the night or to darkness. So we should not be like other people. We should not be sleeping. We should be awake and have self-control.

chapter summaries (@*BibleSummary*)

h 1: Paul, Silas and Timothy, to the Thessalonians. We give thanks for you. Our gospel came in power. Your faith is an example to all.

h 3: We sent Timothy to strengthen you. We warned you that persecution would come. We are encouraged by your faith. May you grow in love.

h 5: The day of the Lord will come like a thief. Let us keep awake. Honour those who lead you. Do not quench the Spirit. Grace be with you.

omething to take away

Ve may have hardships in this life, but we shouldn't lose heart. When we le, we will have everlasting life, and one day God will make everything ght in the world.

2 Thessalonians

What to expect
A letter from Paul and his team
to the church in Thessalonica,
encouraging them in the midst of
persecution.

Chapters 3

Key people
Paul, the church in
Thessalonica.

Timeline

THE BEGINNING · THE PATRIARCHS · IN EGYPT · THE WILDERNESS · PROMISED LAND · THE JUDGES · UNITED KINGDOM · DIVIDED KINGDOM · EXILE IN BABYLON · RETURN FROM EXILE · LIFE OF JESUS · **THE EARLY CHURCH** · THE END

Key passage
2 Thessalonians 1:3,4

*We thank God for you always. And that's what we should do, because you
give us good reason to be thankful: your faith is growing more and more.
And the love that every one of you has for each other is also growing. So
we tell the other churches of God how proud we are of you. We tell them
how you patiently continue to be strong and have faith, even though you
are being persecuted and are suffering many troubles.*

hapter summaries (@*BibleSummary*)

h 1: Paul, Silas and Timothy, to the Thessalonians. We boast of your faith through persecution. The Lord Jesus will appear in vengeance.

h 2: Do not be alarmed about the day of the Lord. First the lawless one will appear, whom Jesus will destroy. Hold fast to our traditions.

omething to take away

rouble will come for Christians. How you deal with it makes the ifference.

1 Timothy

What to expect
A letter from Paul to Timothy, who was leading the church in Ephesus. Paul encourages and instructs him in his leadership.

Chapters 6

Key people
Paul, Timothy.

Timeline

THE BEGINNING
THE PATRIARCHS
IN EGYPT
THE WILDERNESS
PROMISED LAND
THE JUDGES
UNITED KINGDOM
DIVIDED KINGDOM
EXILE IN BABYLON
RETURN FROM EXILE
LIFE OF JESUS
THE EARLY CHURCH
THE END

Key passage
1 Timothy 3:1–5

It is a true statement that anyone whose goal is to serve as an elder has his heart set on a good work. An elder must be such a good man that no one can rightly criticize him. He must be faithful to his wife. He must have self-control and think carefully about the way he lives. He must be respected by others. He must be ready to help people by welcoming them into his home. He must be a good teacher. He must not get drunk or like i fight. He must be gentle and peaceful. He must not be someone who lov money. He must be a good leader of his own family. This means that his children obey him with full respect. If a man does not know how to lead his own family, he will not be able to take care of God's church.

Chapter summaries (*@BibleSummary*)

Ch 1: Paul, to Timothy my son. Stay in Ephesus to correct false teachers. Christ came into the world to save sinners. Glory to God forever!

Ch 3: An overseer must be respectable and manage his family well. Deacons must be dignified and not greedy. Godliness is a great mystery.

Ch 4: In later times some will depart from the faith. Have nothing to do with godless myths. Devote yourself to Scripture and to teaching.

Ch 6: Those who contradict the teaching of Christ understand nothing. The love of money is a root of evil. Fight the good fight of faith.

Something to take away

God will equip us for whatever he has called us to do. If we're called to be leaders, we must live lives that show the gospel.

2 Timothy

What to expect

Another letter from Paul to Timothy, who was leading the church in Ephesus. Paul encourages and instructs him in his leadership.

Chapters 4

Key people
Paul, Timothy.

Timeline

THE BEGINNING
THE PATRIARCHS
IN EGYPT
THE WILDERNESS
PROMISED LAND
THE JUDGES
UNITED KINGDOM
DIVIDED KINGDOM
EXILE IN BABYLON
RETURN FROM EXILE
LIFE OF JESUS
THE EARLY CHURCH
THE END

Key passage
2 Timothy 2:1–6

Timothy, you are a son to me. Be strong in the grace that we have becau we belong to Christ Jesus. What you have heard me teach publicly you should teach to others. Share these teachings with people you can trust. Then they will be able to teach others these same things. As a good sold of Christ Jesus, accept your share of the troubles we have. A soldier wan to please his commanding officer, so he does not spend any time on activities that are not a part of his duty. Athletes in a race must obey all the rules to win. The farmer who works hard deserves the first part of the harvest.

Chapter summaries (@*BibleSummary*)

Ch 1: Paul, to Timothy my son. Fan into flame the gift of God. Share in suffering for the gospel. Hold to the standard of sound teaching.

Ch 2: No soldier gets entangled with civilian affairs. Present yourself to God as an approved worker. Cleanse yourself for honourable use.

Ch 3: In the last days people will be proud and unholy. As for you, continue in what you have learned. All Scripture is inspired by God.

Ch 4: Preach the word in and out of season. I have finished my race. Come to me soon with Mark. Beware of Alexander. The Lord be with you.

Something to take away

We must stay true to what we have been taught about the gospel. And we should pass on what we've learned to others.

Titus

What to expect
A letter from Paul to Titus in Crete, instructing him to teach sound doctrine and to appoint elders.

Chapters 3

Key people
Paul, Titus.

Timeline

THE BEGINNING · THE PATRIARCHS · IN EGYPT · THE WILDERNESS · PROMISED LAND · THE JUDGES · UNITED KINGDOM · DIVIDED KINGDOM · EXILE IN BABYLON · RETURN FROM EXILE · LIFE OF JESUS · **THE EARLY CHURCH** · THE END

Key passage
Titus 1:15,16

To people who are pure, everything is pure. But to those who are full of sin and don't believe, nothing is pure. Really, their thinking has become evil and their consciences have been ruined. They say they know God, but the evil things they do show that they don't accept him. They are disgusting. They refuse to obey God and are not capable of doing anything good.

Chapter summaries (@*BibleSummary*)

Ch 1: Paul, a servant of God, to Titus. I left you in Crete to appoint elders. Deceivers must be silenced. To the impure nothing is pure.

Ch 2: Teach what is consistent with sound doctrine. Men are to be steadfast, women reverent. The grace of God trains us to live godly lives.

Something to take away

Whoever we are and whatever we do, our lives should reflect the gospel.

Philemon

What to expect
A letter from Paul to Philemon, asking him to have mercy on a runaway slave who has become a Christian.

Chapters 1

Key people
Paul, Onesimus, Philemon.

Timeline

THE BEGINNING · THE PATRIARCHS · IN EGYPT · THE WILDERNESS · PROMISED LAND · THE JUDGES · UNITED KINGDOM · DIVIDED KINGDOM · EXILE IN BABYLON · RETURN FROM EXILE · LIFE OF JESUS · **THE EARLY CHURCH** · THE END

Key passage
Philemon 17–19

If you accept me as your friend, then accept Onesimus back. Welcome him like you would welcome me. If he has done any wrong to you or owes you anything, charge that to me. I, Paul, am writing this in my own handwriting: I will pay back anything Onesimus owes. And I will say nothing about what you owe me for your own life.

Chapter summaries (@*BibleSummary*)

Ch 1: Paul, a prisoner, to Philemon. I ask that you receive Onesimus back, not as a slave, but as a brother. Put his wrongs on my account.

Something to take away

Being a Christian will change how we think about one another. Above anything else, we are brothers and sisters in Christ.

Hebrews

What to expect

A letter written to explain how Jesus fulfils the Old Testament law. The author explains that Jesus is the great high priest who offers himself as sacrifice.

Chapters 13

Key people
The writer of Hebrews is unknown.

Timeline

THE BEGINNING · THE PATRIARCHS · IN EGYPT · THE WILDERNESS · PROMISED LAND · THE JUDGES · UNITED KINGDOM · DIVIDED KINGDOM · EXILE IN BABYLON · RETURN FROM EXILE · LIFE OF JESUS · **THE EARLY CHURCH** · THE END

Key passage
Hebrews 9:11,12

But Christ has already come to be the high priest. He is the high priest of the good things we now have. But Christ does not serve in a place like the tent that those other priests served in. He serves in a better place. Unlike that tent, this one is perfect. It was not made by anyone here on earth. It does not belong to this world. Christ entered the Most Holy Place only once – enough for all time. He entered the Most Holy Place by using his own blood, not the blood of goats or young bulls. He entered there and made us free from sin for ever.

Chapter summaries (*@BibleSummary*)

Ch 1: In these last days God spoke by his Son. Of the Son he says, 'Let the angels worship him.' And, 'Your throne, O God, is for ever.'

Ch 2: We must pay closer attention. The author of salvation tasted death for everyone. He was made like us to make atonement for our sins.

Ch 5: Every high priest from among men is subject to weakness. Christ is a high priest in the order of Melchizedek. You still need teaching.

Ch 7: Abraham gave a tithe to Melchizedek, who had no end. Our Lord became a priest through indestructible life. He is always able to save.

Ch 9: The high priest enters the Most Holy Place once a year with blood. Christ entered the true holy place once for all by his own blood.

Ch 10: The law is but a shadow. Animal blood cannot take away sins. Christ offered one sacrifice for ever. So let us hold fast to our hope.

Ch 11: Faith is the proof of hope. By faith the world was made. By faith Abraham obeyed. By faith Moses left Egypt. In faith some suffered.

Ch 12: Let us run the race, looking to Jesus. God is disciplining you as sons. See that no one falls short of grace. Let us worship in awe.

Something to take away

We can have total confidence in what Christ has done at the cross. We never need to look for anyone else to save us.

James

What to expect
A letter from James to the churches, teaching how Christians should live wisely and justly.

Chapters 5

Key people
James.

Timeline

Key passage
James 2:14–17

My brothers and sisters, if a person claims to have faith but does nothing, that faith is worth nothing. Faith like that cannot save anyone. Suppose a brother or sister in Christ comes to you in need of clothes or something to eat. And you say to them, 'God be with you! I hope you stay warm and get plenty to eat,' but you don't give them the things they need. If you don't help them, your words are worthless. It is the same with faith. If it is just faith and nothing more – if it doesn't do anything – it is dead.

Chapter summaries (@*BibleSummary*)

Ch 1: James, to the tribes. Many trials produce perseverance. Riches will fade. Every good gift comes from the Father. Be doers of the word.

Ch 2: If you show partiality to the rich you are committing sin. Act as those who are under the law of liberty. Faith without works is dead.

Ch 4: Your worldly desires cause conflict. Resist the devil, draw near to God. Who are you to judge your neighbour? You boast in arrogance.

Something to take away

Our faith and our actions need to match up. A life of faith is shown in things like caring about the poor and watching how we talk.

1 Peter

What to expect
A letter from Peter to the churches, encouraging the believers to think about Christ's suffering and to live holy lives.

Chapters 5

Key people
Peter.

Timeline

THE BEGINNING
THE PATRIARCHS
IN EGYPT
THE WILDERNESS
PROMISED LAND
THE JUDGES
UNITED KINGDOM
DIVIDED KINGDOM
EXILE IN BABYLON
RETURN FROM EXILE
LIFE OF JESUS
THE EARLY CHURCH
THE END

Key passage
1 Peter 4:1,2

Christ suffered while he was in his body. So you should strengthen yourselves with the same kind of thinking Christ had. The one who accepts suffering in this life has clearly decided to stop sinning. Strengthen yourselves so that you will live your lives here on earth doing what God wants, not the evil things that people want to do.

Chapter summaries (@*BibleSummary*)

Ch 1: Peter, to the diaspora. God has given us new birth through Christ. The prophets told of this grace. So be holy in all your conduct.

Ch 2: You are being built up to be a royal priesthood. Submit to human authority. Live as servants of God. Follow Christ in his suffering.

Ch 3: Wives, submit to your husbands. Husbands, honour your wives. Repay evil with blessing. Christ suffered for sins to bring us to God.

Ch 5: Elders should be examples to the flock. Clothe yourselves with humility. Resist the devil. God will strengthen you. Peace to you all.

Something to take away

Jesus is our example for how to live. He was perfectly holy. We can ask him to help us grow in holiness as well.

2 Peter

What to expect

A letter from Peter to the churches, warning them against false teachers.

Chapters 3

Key people
Peter.

Timeline

THE BEGINNING · THE PATRIARCHS · IN EGYPT · THE WILDERNESS · PROMISED LAND · THE JUDGES · UNITED KINGDOM · DIVIDED KINGDOM · EXILE IN BABYLON · RETURN FROM EXILE · LIFE OF JESUS · **THE EARLY CHURCH** · THE END

Key passage
2 Peter 2:17–19

These false teachers are like springs that have no water. They are like clouds that are blown by a storm. A place in the deepest darkness has been kept for them. They boast with words that mean nothing. They lead people into the trap of sin. They find people who have just escaped from a wrong way of life and lead them back into sin. They do this by using the evil things people want to do in their human weakness. These false teachers promise those people freedom, but they themselves are not free. They are slaves to a mind that has been ruined by sin. Yes, people are slaves to anything that controls them.

Chapter summaries (*@BibleSummary*)

Ch 1: Peter, to those of faith. God has given us great promises. So supplement faith with virtue and love. We were eyewitnesses of Christ.

Ch 2: False teachers will arise. If God did not spare angels then he knows how to punish the unrighteous. They are slaves of corruption.

Ch 3: Scoffers will say, 'Where is his return?' The Lord is not slow, but patient. Untaught people twist the Scriptures. Grow in Christ.

Something to take away

Not everyone who claims to teach the truth can be trusted. We shouldn't listen to those who question whether Christ is really coming back.

1 John

What to expect

A letter from John to the churches, encouraging the believers to abide in Christ and love one another.

Chapters 5

Key people
John.

Timeline

THE BEGINNING
THE PATRIARCHS
IN EGYPT
THE WILDERNESS
PROMISED LAND
THE JUDGES
UNITED KINGDOM
DIVIDED KINGDOM
EXILE IN BABYLON
RETURN FROM EXILE
LIFE OF JESUS
THE EARLY CHURCH
THE END

Key passage
1 John 4:7–10

Dear friends, we should love each other, because love comes from God. Everyone who loves has become God's child. And so everyone who loves knows God. Anyone who does not love does not know God, because God is love. This is how God showed his love to us: he sent his only Son into the world to give us life through him. True love is God's love for us, not our love for God. He sent his Son as the way to take away our sins.

Chapter summaries (*@BibleSummary*)

Ch 1: We have seen and proclaim to you the Word of life. God is light. If we walk in the light, the blood of Jesus cleanses us from all sin.

Ch 3: We are God's children. Those born of God do not sin. We should love one another. We know love because he laid down his life for us.

Ch 4: Any spirit that confesses Christ is of God. God is love. He sent his Son as a sacrifice for sins. If we live in love, God lives in us.

Ch 5: Anyone born of God overcomes the world. The Spirit, water and blood all testify. God gave us eternal life in his Son. Keep from idols.

Something to take away

At the heart of everything, God has shown his love for us in Christ. We should love one another with that same love.

2 John

What to expect
A letter from John to the churches, warning them not to welcome false teachers.

Chapters 1

Key people
John, the lady.

Timeline

THE BEGINNING · THE PATRIARCHS · IN EGYPT · THE WILDERNESS · PROMISED LAND · THE JUDGES · UNITED KINGDOM · DIVIDED KINGDOM · EXILE IN BABYLON · RETURN FROM EXILE · LIFE OF JESUS · **THE EARLY CHURCH** · THE END

Key passage
2 John 9–11

Everyone must continue to follow only the teaching about Christ. Whoever changes that teaching does not have God. But whoever continues to follow the teaching about Christ has both the Father and his Son. Don't accept those who come to you but do not bring this teaching. Don't invite them into your house. Don't welcome them in any way. If you do, you are helping them with their evil work.

Chapter summaries (*@BibleSummary*)

Ch 1: The elder, to the elect lady. Let us love one another as the Father commands. Do not welcome false teachers. I hope to come to you.

Something to take away

It matters who we allow to teach us and speak into our lives.

3 John

What to expect
A letter from John to Gaius, encouraging him in his faith.

Chapters 1

Key people
John, Gaius.

Timeline

THE BEGINNING · THE PATRIARCHS · IN EGYPT · THE WILDERNESS · PROMISED LAND · THE JUDGES · UNITED KINGDOM · DIVIDED KINGDOM · EXILE IN BABYLON · RETURN FROM EXILE · LIFE OF JESUS · **THE EARLY CHURCH** · THE END

Key passage
3 John 2–4

My dear friend, I know that you are doing well spiritually. So I pray that everything else is going well with you and that you are enjoying good health. Some believers came and told me about the truth in your life. They told me that you continue to follow the way of truth. This made me very happy. It always gives me the greatest joy when I hear that my children are following the way of truth.

Chapter summaries (@*BibleSummary*)

Ch 1: The elder, to beloved Gaius. I was overjoyed to hear of your faithfulness. Diotrephes spreads false charges. I hope to see you soon.

Something to take away

It's good to encourage one another in the faith. Is there someone you could encourage today?

Jude

What to expect

A letter from Jude to the believers, warning against those who have turned grace into an excuse to keep on sinning.

Chapters 1

Key people
Jude.

Timeline

THE BEGINNING
THE PATRIARCHS
IN EGYPT
THE WILDERNESS
PROMISED LAND
THE JUDGES
UNITED KINGDOM
DIVIDED KINGDOM
EXILE IN BABYLON
RETURN FROM EXILE
LIFE OF JESUS
THE EARLY CHURCH
THE END

Key passage
Jude 3,4

Dear friends, I wanted very much to write to you about the salvation we all share together. But I felt the need to write to you about something else: I want to encourage you to fight hard for the faith that God gave his holy people. God gave this faith once, and it is good for all time. Some people have secretly entered your group. These people have already been judged guilty for what they are doing. Long ago the prophets wrote about them. They are against God. They have used the grace of our God in the wrong way – to do sinful things. They refuse to follow Jesus Christ, our only Master and Lord.

Jude

Chapter summaries (*@BibleSummary*)

Ch 1: Jude, to the elect. Ungodly people pervert grace into sensuality. They are judged as twice-dead trees. Build yourselves up in faith.

Something to take away
We should keep away from anyone who teaches that sin is OK.

Revelation

What to expect

A vision of the end of the world. The Christians were facing persecution under the Roman Empire. Revelation assures us that God will overcome Satan in the end.

Chapters 22

Key people
John, the seven churches in Asia Minor, Jesus.

Timeline

THE BEGINNING
THE PATRIARCHS
IN EGYPT
THE WILDERNESS
PROMISED LAND
THE JUDGES
UNITED KINGDOM
DIVIDED KINGDOM
EXILE IN BABYLON
RETURN FROM EXILE
LIFE OF JESUS
THE EARLY CHURCH
THE END

Key passage
Revelation 21:1–5a

Then I saw a new heaven and a new earth. The first heaven and the first earth had disappeared. Now there was no sea. And I saw the holy city, the new Jerusalem, coming down out of heaven from God. It was prepared like a bride dressed for her husband.

I heard a loud voice from the throne. It said, 'Now God's home is with people. He will live with them. They will be his people. God himself will be with them and will be their God. He will wipe away every tear from their eyes. There will be no more death, sadness, crying or pain. All the old ways are gone.'

The one who was sitting on the throne said, 'Look, I am making everything new!'

Chapter summaries (*@BibleSummary*)

Ch 1: The revelation of Jesus Christ to John. A voice said, 'Write to the churches.' I saw one like a son of man, his face was like the sun.

Ch 4: I saw one seated on the throne in heaven. The four living creatures say, 'Holy, holy, holy.' The elders say, 'You created all things.'

Ch 5: A Lamb standing as though slain took the scroll with seven seals. The creatures, elders and myriad angels sang, 'Worthy is the Lamb!'

Ch 7: The 144,000 were sealed from the tribes. A multitude cried, 'Salvation belongs to our God.' An elder said, 'God will wipe every tear.'

Ch 11: The two witnesses will prophesy until the beast kills them. At the seventh trumpet, loud voices said, 'Our God shall reign for ever.'

Ch 13: I saw a beast rising out of the sea. It spoke blasphemy against God. Another beast rose and gave everyone a mark. Its number is 666.

Ch 14: I saw the Lamb in Zion with the 144,000. Angels said, 'The hour of judgement has come.' The earth was reaped with a sharp sickle.

Ch 16: The bowls of wrath were poured out. The seas turned to blood, darkness fell, the kings gathered at Armageddon and the earth quaked.

Ch 17: I saw a prostitute on a beast with seven heads and ten horns. An angel said, 'The heads and horns are kings. The Lamb will conquer.'

Revelation

Ch 19: A multitude cried, 'Hallelujah! The Lord reigns.' The Word of God led the armies of heaven. The beast was cast into the lake of fire.

Ch 20: Satan was bound and the martyrs reigned with Christ for 1,000 years. Then Satan was cast into the lake of fire. The dead were judged.

Ch 21: I saw a new heaven and earth. A voice said, 'God dwells with his people.' An angel showed me the new Jerusalem. Its lamp is the Lamb.

Ch 22: The river of life flows from the throne of God. 'Behold, I am coming soon. I am the beginning and the end.' Amen. Come, Lord Jesus!

Something to take away

God's plan will succeed! From the beginning he wanted to be in perfect relationship with his people, and in the end that's exactly how it will be.